# THE CIVIL WAR SONGBOOK

## Complete Original Sheet Music for 37 Songs

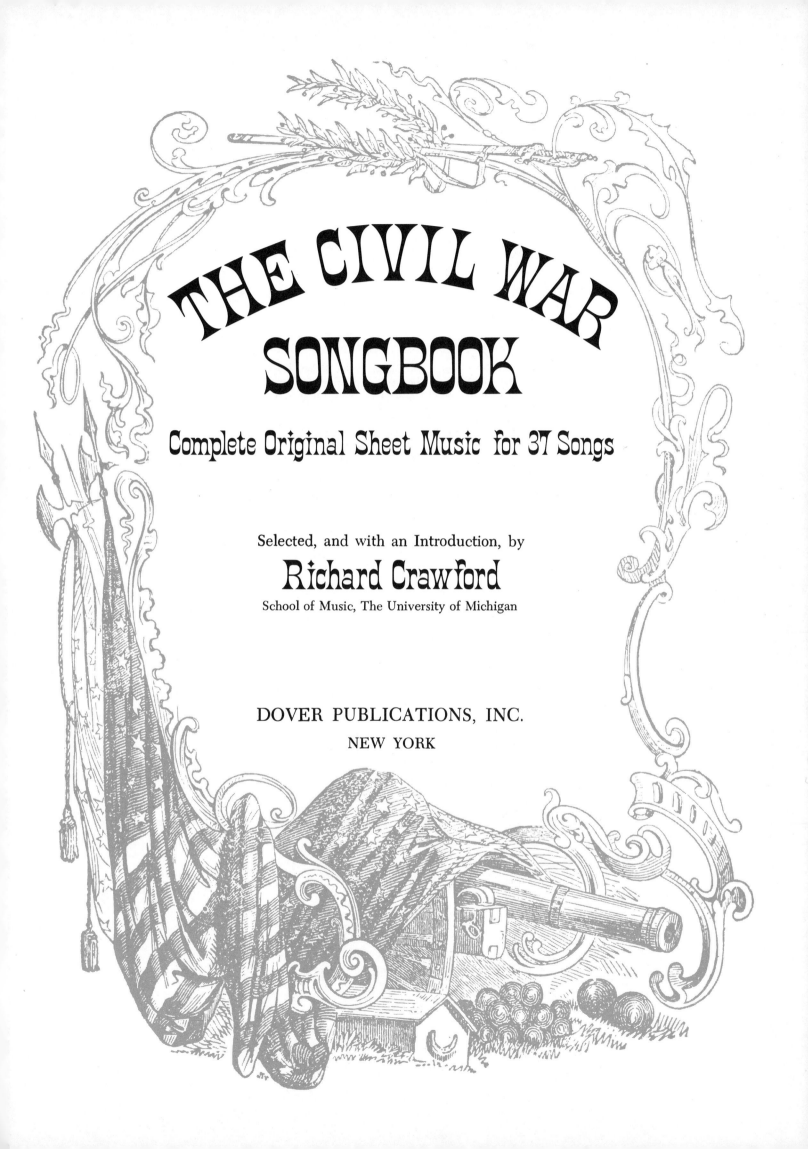

# THE CIVIL WAR SONGBOOK

## Complete Original Sheet Music for 37 Songs

Selected, and with an Introduction, by

### Richard Crawford

School of Music, The University of Michigan

DOVER PUBLICATIONS, INC.

NEW YORK

## ACKNOWLEDGMENTS

Editor and publisher are grateful to the William Clements Library, University of Michigan, Ann Arbor, for supplying reproduction copy of the following songs in their collection: "The Southrons' Chaunt of Defiance," "The Soldier's Return," "The Dying Volunteer," "Bear Gently, So Gently, the Roughly Made Bier," "The New Emancipation Song" and "We Are Coming from the Cotton Fields."

Mr. Lester S. Levy made his copy of "Battle Hymn of the Republic" available to us.

All the other songs are reproduced directly from the original sheet music lent by the eminent collector William Lloyd Keepers, without whose cooperation this book would not have been possible.

Published in Canada by General Publishing Company, Ltd., 30 Lesmill Road, Don Mills, Toronto, Ontario.

Published in the United Kingdom by Constable and Company, Ltd., 10 Orange Street, London WC2H 7EG.

*The Civil War Songbook: Complete Original Sheet Music for 37 Songs* is a new work, first published by Dover Publications, Inc., in 1977.

*International Standard Book Number: 0-486-23422-3*
*Library of Congress Catalog Card Number: 76-20846*

Manufactured in the United States of America
Dover Publications, Inc.
180 Varick Street
New York, N.Y. 10014

# Introduction

The music of the American Civil War has many tales to tell. Its background is implicitly religious, and the combatants never doubt that they deserve God's blessing. It celebrates lofty political ideals: union and states' rights. It commemorates heroes and martyrs. It struts exultantly in victory and mourns defeat. It glimpses human dramas behind the fighting lines: the wife urges her husband to battle; the mother weeps for her slain son; the dying soldier clings to memories of home.

Of all the events in American history, perhaps none was reflected in song with such innocent vigor as the Civil War, and none can claim to have given birth to more effective or enduring popular pieces. Music inspired by the Civil War ranges from stirring parade music for bands and virtuosic piano fantasies for concert audiences, through marches and songs for the home performer, to ballads based on traditional tunes and transmitted orally rather than in print. The present volume is devoted to songs written for sheet-music circulation and finding a home in the American parlor. Reprinted here are a few representative pieces from a sizable repertory composed mostly for those who did not fight the War Between the States but who stayed home. It was to their hopes and fears that the music was addressed, and their beliefs, values and musical tastes shaped it. If this collection has its own tale to tell, the tale might be called: The American Sheet-Music Industry and American Domestic Sensibility During the Civil War, or How The War Felt From The Piano Stool.

The tale cannot be appreciated without some consideration of the American sheet-music industry. Under way by the last decade of the eighteenth century, the sheet-music industry had by 1825 established itself firmly in the major cities of the eastern seaboard: Boston, New York, Philadelphia, Baltimore. A typical piece of sheet music of this early period was a two-page affair, printed on facing pages from an engraved pewter or copper plate, and of suitable size to be set on the rack of a keyboard instrument, where it could be seen by two or more performers if need be. During the years between 1825 and the Civil War the sheet-music business reached a kind of commercial maturity. Lithography, in which an image could be transferred cheaply from a stone to paper, made illustrated covers more prevalent. (A song introduced by an attractive picture to adorn the parlor became that much more a bargain.) Westward expansion brought sheet-music publishers to Pittsburgh, Cleveland, Detroit, Louisville, Chicago and St. Louis, as well as many smaller towns. The improvement of transportation via railroads and canals helped to create distribution networks for sheet music, so that the purchaser had an ever-widening assortment to choose from, as well as access to the most up-to-date selections, even if they were originally printed hundreds of miles away. Finally, musical-instrument makers kept pace with the growth of the sheet-music business, and the two fed each other in a kind of symbiotic cycle. By the time of the Civil War American piano makers, according to Arthur Loesser's *Men, Women and Pianos*, were producing more than 20,000 pianos a year for a population of some 31,000,000, and merchandisers were giving installment terms to buyers, even down to the cheaper models which sold for around $300. Thus, in the years prior to the War, American musical commerce made a concerted and by all accounts successful assault on the American parlor.

From the first the American sheet-music industry had printed mostly imported compositions, and even at mid-century much of its music was by popular European composers. The presses of London, Paris, Leipzig and other European centers were major sources. Songs and salon pieces by the likes of William Wallace, or Henri Herz, or Stephen Heller could be copied by American publishers and sold here without royalty fee. (International copyright designed to stop such piracy was not enacted until the very end of the century.) European operas, especially Italian, were another prime source for songs and instrumental pieces, often potpourris and variations. But ever more important was the music of domestic composers. By the 1840s there had developed, apparently upon European models, several genres of simple American popular music. The parlor song of the type written by the Englishman Henry Russell or by Stephen Foster was a strophic piece with a singable diatonic melody and an uncomplicated piano accompaniment; it flourished throughout the latter part of the century and on into the present one. Its counterpart for piano was the character piece—usually a short dance or march, descriptively titled, with several repeated strains. Also popular were sets of piano variations, in which a tune—hopefully well-known—was presented and then varied and embellished in a succession of parallel restatements. Another genre popular from the 1840s and not derived from European practice was the songs and dances of blackface minstrelsy. Based upon theatrical whites' observation of the musical practices of plantation and city blacks, the minstrel-show music published in sheets introduced a note of earthy irreverence into the American parlor.

When the Civil War broke out in 1861 the American sheet-music industry was ready, artistically and technologically, to capitalize on it. Composers and lyricists abounded who could supply topical songs with near-electric speed. Music could be engraved, printed and distributed swiftly by experienced, expert publishers. (George F. Root's "The First Gun Is Fired! May God Protect the Right!" was on sale April 15, 1861, three days after Fort Sumter was fired upon.) Nor was this condition exclusive to the highly organized commercial North. Richard Harwell's *Confederate Music*, which documents the flourishing sheet-music industry of the South, notes that because songs were "cheap to produce" and required little capital investment by the publishers, "it is hardly surprising that the pieces of music bearing Confederate imprints are more than five times the number of novels, plays, and other books of pleasure" (p. 4).

For the sheet-music industry, the Civil War was a time of excitement and glory and profit. Demand for the standard parlor repertory, already brisk, was now supplemented by a demand for war music. Art, patriotism and commerce—usually uneasy bedfellows—were fused by the conflict, producing music that a wide spectrum of society on both sides found useful, perhaps even edifying. Civil War parlor music was topical art: it identified and fixed images of meaning for citizens who were seeing their world changed by circumstances beyond their imagination. The patriotic appeal lifted the matter, or at least seemed to, to a higher, more public plane, so that the citizen who sang or heard patriotic music could tingle for a cause rather than merely for himself. And behind the maelstrom of emotion churned to the surface by the conflict, standing to profit by it, yet anxious to believe that his success served his country's greater good, stood the publisher/author/composer. The fusion apparently came unstuck after peace returned, for Root & Cady's *Song Messenger Extra* (May 1869) complained: "since the war, neither we nor any other American publishers, have made any great hits in sheet music." Yet while art, patriotism and commerce were fused by the War's unrecoverable circumstances, a sheet-music repertory of great size and timeliness was created.

Certain war-related topics lent themselves naturally to musical treatment, and this collection is organized according to those topics: Patriotic Songs, The Soldiering Life, Battlefield Deaths, Domestic Scenes and Emancipation Songs. Other topics are conspicuous by their absence. For example, though unrest about political leaders frequently boiled to the surface in Civil War journalism, and though the conduct of the war was the subject of bitter public wrangling for most of its duration, I have found no antiwar songs, nor indeed any songs on either side anti anything except the declared enemy. Nothing with the slightest hint of the subversive or even the faintly controversial seems to have made its way into the repertory; most likely commercial conventions, not fear of censorship, caused this ideological blandness.

*Patriotic Songs.* A group of songs served during the war as the focus for national sentiment, including two all-time American favorites, "Dixie" ("Dixie's Land") and the "Battle Hymn of the Republic." Perhaps it would be more accurate to call this group of songs chauvinistic rather than patriotic. Patriotism connotes a disinterested self-sacrificing concern for the well-being of one's country, but there was little room for restraint in this repertory. Even patriotic songs that, like "Dixie," are not exaggeratedly bellicose came to symbolize blind enthusiasm for one side and hysterical hatred for the other.

Musical borrowing is an accepted popular technique, and of the war's most famous patriotic songs, only Root's "The Battle Cry of Freedom" had both words and music freshly composed with an ultimately patriotic purpose in mind. The "Battle Hymn of the Republic" had earlier been sung as

"John Brown's Body" to a Sunday School hymn tune; the Southern favorite, Emmett's "Dixie," had been a Northern blackface minstrel song; Macarthy's "The Bonnie Blue Flag" was set to a traditional song called "The Irish Jaunting Car"; and the German Christmas song "O Tannenbaum" provided the tune for "Maryland, My Maryland!" All of these pieces were frequently parodied, each side issuing the other's favorites with texts altered appropriately. "The Southrons' Chaunt of Defiance" by Blackmar illustrates the uncompromising spirit expressed by most of the patriotic songs on both sides. Given the climate of moral totalism fostered by the Civil War, it is not surprising that the moderate and pragmatic Abraham Lincoln, commonly condemned as a vacillator, had to be assassinated before the sheet-music industry canonized him as an official hero.

*The Soldiering Life.* Parlor music gave noncombatants a sizable if somewhat oblique dose of the "realities" of the soldier's life, in and out of battle. Bluff marching songs exuding masculine fellowship are common, but there are also a number of more meditative pieces. (The navy's role in the war received no significant musical commemoration.)

The soldier's life, as depicted in Civil War parlor music, had considerable range. Camaraderie was not the least of the recruit's rewards. James Sloan Gibbons' poem "We Are Coming Father Abraham, Three Hundred Thousand More" was written in response to Lincoln's call for more troops, the pounding accents of its lengthy lines suggesting music to at least eight different composers, though only Emerson's setting, with its erroneous attribution of the words to Bryant, is printed here. (Some settings doubled the call to 600,000 more.) Gibbons' vision showed a horde of recruits responding to the President's order as if to a religious summons, and its cumulative force as a song is powerful. A sunnier, less compulsive camaraderie is pictured in Work's "Marching Through Georgia," as Sherman's veterans swing toward the sea under the summer sun of 1864. (Southerners since the war have despised Work's song, a reminder of the Union Army's destruction of their land.) Root's unique "Who'll Save the Left?" is as close as American composers of Civil War parlor music ever got to an operatic *scena*, and his "Tramp! Tramp! Tramp!" reflects, if rather eupeptically, another contingency of the soldier's life: the possibility of capture. Nor does the repertory ignore the introspective. Root's "Just Before the Battle, Mother"—whose popularity, incidentally, inspired a sequel, "Just After the Battle"—may seem musically and poetically insipid, but its emotional framework is not farfetched. Thomas' "The Soldier's Return," in which the recruit imagines himself going home to his waiting sweetheart, is more operatically forceful and musically extroverted. Kittredge's elegiac "Tenting on the Old Camp Ground" and Hewitt's ironic and lovely "All Quiet Along the Potomac To-Night"—a Southern song published in the North as "The Picket's Guard" with slightly changed text—are still capable of touching a responsive chord. Finally, what Robert Penn Warren has called the "marmoreal rigidity" of Civil War thinking is illustrated both by Beckel's "The Grant Pill" with its decisive refrain of "Unconditional Surrender!" and by "O I'm a Good Old Rebel," a sour Southern ballad based on the folksong "Joe Bowers." The latter exemplifies the oral tradition, which supplied much of the music the soldiers themselves sang. What is remarkable about "O I'm a Good Old Rebel" is that so rough a piece was written down and harmonized and issued in sheet-music form for the parlor.

*Battlefield Deaths.* More than 600,000 Americans were killed in the Civil War, and civilians of all ages were far more prone to sudden fatal illness than twentieth-century Americans. Faced with death as a common fact of existence, the nineteenth century did not share our prudery about the subject. A man's life was apt to be seen as a story written by God. As the end of the story, the deathbed utterance was a denouement, and such scenes were favorites in drama and song. In Civil War parlor music the dying hero is often given time to say his piece, and the piece unfailingly turns out to be appropriate as a set of last words.

It is in the songs about battlefield deaths and domestic scenes that the sentimental strain is worked most freely. Clark's "The Children of the Battle Field," like a fair number of war pieces, was inspired by a poignant incident reported in the press. The story of the song's genesis appears with the piece, together with a stylized likeness of the children whose picture their soldier father grasped when his body was found on the Gettysburg field. Several songs are devoted to dying words of the wounded. In Sontag's "Comrades, I Am Dying!" the soldier urges his companions back to the battle then sees a vision of his late mother descending from the clouds to take his soul back with her. Hays's "The Drummer Boy of Shiloh" pictures a dying youth—supported on his knees by a soldier and surrounded by a group of soldier comrades as the battle rages in the background—who makes his last living act a prayer. Another drummer, the "Little Major" of Work's song, does not fare so well, dying alone and unattended, his request for water brushed aside with a callous "Nothing but a wounded drummer." Gumpert's "The Dying Volunteer" pictures one of the war's first fatalities, and here the slain man dies with thoughts of his country on his lips; the echo refrain, "All hail to the Stars and Stripes!," coupled with the use of the minor mode—very rare in parlor songs—gives this song an unusual expressive impact. Finally, Mathias' "Bear Gently, So Gently, the Roughly Made Bier" depicts a camp burial, with much being made over the corpse, which is viewed, kissed, blessed and interred before the soldier's comrades return to battle.

*Domestic Scenes.* The home bore much of the War's psychic impact, and a good deal of the War's music portrays the feelings of those who waited there for their absent sons and brothers and husbands. The domestic songs complement the songs about the soldiering life. By picturing the anxious, lonely families the soldiers left behind, they dramatize the Civil War as a conflict of volunteers, not professional military men. The domestic landscape, generally maudlin, is brightened by an occasional joke piece or even by jaunty optimism, as in a song like "When Johnny Comes Marching Home."

Mother's presence hovers over almost all of the domestic songs. Covert's "Can I Go, Dearest Mother?" is a prospective recruit's impassioned plea for maternal blessing before he enlists. "Ah! the many cruel fancies / Ever in my brain," says one of the verses of Tucker's "Weeping, Sad and Lonely"—also called "When This Cruel War Is Over"—and this could be taken as a pervasive refrain for the domestic anxiousness so frequently expressed. In Root's "O Come You from the Battle-Field?," a "Dialogue duett" for soprano and tenor, a soldier tells an anxious mother of her son's bravery and safety: he has earned a medal and a pension for saving an officer's life. The refrain of this song, ending "All sorrows now are o'er," speaks the wish, also expressed in "When Johnny Comes Marching Home," that the war's end will bring back the tranquility of prewar days, which from a wartime perspective can be remembered euphorically. Death struck many homes, and in Root's "The Vacant Chair" a soldier's place at the Thanksgiving table stands unoccupied, the family consoled only by knowing that he has fallen bravely in battle. The same note of resignation pervades Work's "Brave Boys Are They!" as homebound women meditate on the death awaiting some of their menfolk. More melodramatic in tone is Roefs's "Mother Is the Battle Over?," in which a child gradually infers from Mother's doleful silence and tear-stained face that Father will not be coming home from the wars. Yet the War also produced a host of comic songs. Work's "Grafted into the Army" shows an American mother reacting to the unfamiliar vocabulary of her son's new military vocation with a flood of malaprops. And the undignified circumstances of Jefferson Davis' postwar capture—he tried to escape arrest in women's dress—are mocked in Tucker's jovial "Jeff in Petticoats." Light spirits too had a place in the parlor.

*Emancipation Songs.* Although slavery more than anything else touched off the Civil War, emancipation, according to historians, was at first a military ploy, only later being recognized as the basis for a new social order. Whites and blacks are at this writing still working to follow Lincoln's injunction to "live themselves out of their old relation with each other." As might be expected, Civil War parlor music concentrates not on this aspect of emancipation, nor on the tragic fate of many black refugees after freedom was declared, but instead on the national government's benevolence in granting slaves their freedom and upon the blacks' naïve joy at their release from bondage.

The singing Hutchinson Family had worked long for abolition, and Mrs. Parkhurst's "The New Emancipation Song" was given out as a piece sung by them. Rather than a narrative the song is a kind of litany, with a very brief verse and a simple repetitive chorus; like the religious camp-meeting song, this is a piece that one can imagine sung responsorially between a leader (verse) and an audience (chorus). Root's "Glory! Glory! or The Little Octoroon" is musically attractive but also somewhat puzzling. Its vaulting, declamatory tune hardly seems consonant with the tenderness of its subject. (And history leaves room to wonder how many biracial children were welcomed so kindly at Union army camps.) Work's dialect song "Kingdom Coming" draws on the tradition of blackface humor developed in the minstrel shows. French's "Sixty-Three Is the Jubilee," if somewhat smoother musically than much minstrel music, still has moments of syncopated rhythmic vigor and a bumptiousness that suggests the vernacular toughness of the minstrel strain. Finally, the tune of "We Are Coming from the Cotton Fields," by J. C. Wallace, combines syncopation, melodic leaps and march-like dotted rhythms, set to a heartfelt text expressing the freedmen's acceptance of their new life.

As this collection demonstrates, the parlor music of the Civil War is rooted in metrical strophic poetry. In most songs the textual phrase generates the musical phrase. Word repetition is relatively infrequent; so is melismatic writing (many notes on one syllable). Therefore, the musical phrase generally reflects the accent pattern of the phrase of text to which it is set, and the symmetry of the text leads to a corresponding musical tidiness: a predictable succession of antecedent and consequent phrases. After the phrase the next basic musical unit is the stanza, and each stanza is usually comprised of an even number of lines: four or six or eight. In many songs each stanza or "verse" is followed by a refrain or "chorus," a concluding section in which text and music are unchanging. Typically the verses are set for solo voice and the refrain is harmonized for soprano, alto, tenor and bass. Thus, most songs are obsessively regular and repetitive in form: phrases are symmetrical, each stanza is sung to the same music, and refrains repeat both text and music.

The musical idiom of Civil War parlor music, like the musical structure, aims at easy comprehensibility. Melodic lines are written for the normal amateur voice, apparently to provide a singable tune to which the text can be clearly declaimed. The harmony moves generally with smoothness through a very restricted range of possibilities. Though many of the texts are lugubrious, the mode almost always remains major. The repertory is by no means free of "expressive" musical effects, especially harmonic devices supporting ominous textual references. The pervading musical idiom in most pieces, however, is so decisively bland that these moments of musical "intensity" are likely to seem more comic than effective.

The sensibility of the Civil War parlor is so far removed from that of the present day that much of the music in this collection may seem absurd. Indeed an often unsympathetic image of reality presents itself here. Ideology is absolute. Ambiguities and measured feelings are not expressed, and the motive of revenge is never far below the surface in patriotic music. A kind of connoisseurship of grief and pain is displayed, and sentimentality —the cultivation of emotion for its own sake— washes over much of the repertory. The war as felt from the piano stool loses its brutality; it is transformed and domesticated to correspond with the atmosphere of gentility that pervaded the American parlor in prewar days and that continued to dominate it afterwards. The transformation defines its cultural role: to mediate between the war's reality and the vision of reality that the population could accept and live with. Civil War parlor music was a kind of rite that helped citizens to deal with events that changed their lives beyond their powers of psychological adjustment. Playing and singing are physical pursuits, and the act of playing and singing about events in one's life is an ancient human ritual. As musically weak and commercially debased as some Civil War parlor pieces may be, it is reading only part of the story to condemn the repertory on aesthetic grounds, as if it were merely a collection of moral and social emblems of "bad taste" rather than a reflection of one of man's healthier reactions to experience: the making of music about it.

# Composers

Biographical data on some of the composers can be found through the *Bio-Bibliographical Index of Musicians in the United States,* 2nd ed. (Washington: Pan American Union, 1956; reprinted, New York: Da Capo Press, 1971). Additional information is also in Nicholas Slonimsky, *Baker's Biographical Dictionary of Musicians,* 5th ed. with Supplement (New York: G. Schirmer, 1971), Kenneth A. Bernard, *Lincoln and the Music of the Civil War* (Caldwell, Idaho: Caxton, 1966) and Richard Harwell, *Confederate Music* (Chapel Hill: University of North Carolina Press, 1950). There are also useful data in Richard Jackson, *Popular Songs of Nineteenth-Century America* (New York: Dover, 1976). The entries below refer to these items as follows: *Bio-Bibliographical Index,* (B); *Baker's,* (Ba); Bernard, (Be); Harwell, (H); Jackson, (J). No effort has been made to trace composers beyond these sources; composers for whom no information has been found are not listed.

BECKEL, JAMES COX (1811–?): Philadelphia organist, composed sacred music and an organ method, and also arranged songs; still alive and musically active in the 1880s. (B)

BLACKMAR, ARMAND EDWARD (1826–88): native of Vermont who moved to Ohio, graduated from Western Reserve College (1845), and then moved South; a composer and music dealer, Blackmar also published music in Augusta, Vicksburg, Mobile and San Francisco, as well as New Orleans, his base of operations through the war. (H)

CLARK, JAMES GOWDY (1830–97).

EMERSON, LUTHER ORLANDO (1820–1915): composer, teacher, conductor and compiler of songbooks and sacred music collections; born in Parsonsfield, Maine, and died in Hyde Park, Massachusetts. (Ba)

EMMETT, DANIEL DECATUR (1815–1904): composer, lyricist and performer who spent much of his career in blackface minstrelsy; he was born in Mount Vernon, Ohio, and he died there. (Ba)

GILMORE, PATRICK SARSFIELD (1829–92): native of Ireland who emigrated to Boston, organizing Gilmore's Band (1859) and two huge musical festivals (1869, 1872); composed songs and military pieces, and also arranged music for band; died in St. Louis. (Ba)

HAYS, WILLIAM SHAKESPEARE (1837–1907): Louisville songwriter and newspaperman; published more than 300 songs, many of which enjoyed wide sheet-music sale. (Ba)

HEWITT, JOHN HILL (1801–90): son of James Hewitt, a leading immigrant professional musician; had an itinerant career as a composer (more than 300 songs), poet and theatrical entrepreneur; born in New York, he spent the Civil War in the Confederacy and died in Baltimore. (H)

KITTREDGE, WALTER (1834–1905): New Hampshire singer, composer and lecturer; born in Reed's Ferry, buried at Merrimack near the place of his death; spent part of his public career singing with the Hutchinson Family. (Be)

LAMBERT, LOUIS: pseudonym for Gilmore, Patrick Sarsfield, q.v.

MACARTHY, HARRY (1834–88): billed himself as "the Arkansas comedian"; born in England; an actor and singer, he wrote Confederate songs early in the war, then went North before it was over; died in Oakland, California. (H)

PARKHURST, MRS. E. A.: later known as Mrs. Duer.

ROOT, GEORGE FREDERICK (1820–95): born in Sheffield, Massachusetts; died in Maine; teacher, composer and tastemaker—a partner in the successful Chicago firm of Root & Cady, which specialized in sheet music and tune books for schools and churches. (Ba)

THOMAS, JOHN ROGERS (1829–96): native of Wales; settled in New York, where he worked as a professional singer of opera and oratorio and a composer of songs. (B)

TUCKER, HENRY: composer of numerous popular songs, including the standard "Sweet Genevieve." (J)

WORK, HENRY CLAY (1832–84): born in Middletown, Connecticut, and died in Hartford, but spent much of his life as a printer in Chicago and New York; most of the 70-odd songs he published were written in the 1860s. (Ba)

# Books for Further Reference

Epstein, Dena J. *Music Publishing in Chicago Before 1871: The Firm of Root & Cady, 1858–1871.* Detroit: Information Coordinators, Inc., 1969.

Glass, Paul, and Louis C. Singer. *Singing Soldiers: A History of the Civil War in Song.* New York: Da Capo, 1975 (orig. pub. 1964 as *The Spirit of the Sixties*).

Heaps, Willard A., and Porter W. Heaps. *The Singing Sixties.* Norman: University of Oklahoma Press, 1960.

Silber, Irwin. *Songs of the Civil War.* New York: Columbia University Press, 1960.

# Contents

# THE Battle-Cry of Freedom.

Words & Music by

## GEO. F. ROOT.

Published by ROOT & CADY 95 Clark St.
CHICAGO.

S. BRAINARD & CO.,—CLEVELAND.     H. TOLMAN & CO.—BOSTON     H. N. HEMPSTED—MILWAUKEE

Entered according to act of Congress A.D. 1862 by Root & Cady in the Clerk's Office of the District Court for the North⁰ Dist. of Illinois.

# THE
# BATTLE CRY OF FREEDOM.

GEO. F. ROOT.

INTRODUCTION

1. Yes we'll ral- -ly round the flag, boys, we'll
2. We are spring-ing to the call for Three
3. We will wel- -come to our num- -bers the
4. So we're spring-ing to the call from the

ral ly once a gain, Shout-ing the bat-tle-cry of Free- -dom, We will
Hundred Thou-sand more, Shout-ing the bat-tle-cry of Free- -dom, And we'll
loy-al true and brave, Shout-ing the bat-tle-cry of Free- -dom, And al-
East and from the West, Shout-ing the bat-tle-cry of Free- -dom, And we'll

2

ral-ly from the hill-side we'll gath-er from the plain, Shout-ing the bat-tle-cry of
fill the va-cant ranks of our broth-ers gone be-fore, Shout-ing the bat-tle-cry of
tho' he may be poor he shall nev-er be a slave, Shout-ing the bat-tle-cry of
hurl the reb-el crew from the land we love the best, Shout-ing the bat-tle-cry of

CHORUS

Fortssimo.

AIR

Free- -dom.    The Un- -ion for-ev-er, Hur- -rah boys, hur-rah!

ALTO

The Un- -ion for-ev-er, Hur- -rah boys, hur-rah!

TENOR

The Un- -ion for-ev-er, Hur- -rah boys, hur-rah!

BASE

PIANO

Down with the Trai-tor, Up with the Star; While we ral-ly round the flag, boys,

Down with the Trai-tor, Up with the Star; While we ral-ly round the flag, boys,

Down with the Trai-tor, Up with the Star; While we ral-ly round the flag, boys,

Ral-ly once a-gain, Shout-ing the bat-tle--cry of Free--dom.

Ral-ly once a-gain, Shout-ing the bat-tle--cry of Free--dom.

Ral-ly once a-gain, Shout-ing the bat-tle--cry of Free--dom.

# BATTLE HYMN OF THE REPUBLIC

Adapted to the favorite Melody

of

## "Glory, Hallelujah,"

WRITTEN BY

## Mrs. Dr. S. G. Howe,

FOR THE

## ATLANTIC MONTHLY.

BOSTON.
Published by Oliver Ditson & Co. 277 Washington St.

Firth Pond & Co.    J. Church Jr.    J. C. Haynes & Co.    J. E. Gould    C. C. Clapp & Co.
N. York.              Cin.              Boston              Philad^a         Boston.

# BATTLE HYMN OF THE REPUBLIC.

Mine eyes have seen the glo-ry of the coming of the Lord: He is

trampling out the vintage where the grapes of wrath are stored; He hath loosed the fateful lightning of His

ter - ri-ble swift sword: His truth is march-ing on.

Glo - ry! Glo-ry Hal-le-lu - jah! Glo-ry! Glory! Glory Halle - lu - jah!

Glo - ry! Glo-ry Hal-le-lu - jah! Glo-ry! Glory! Glory Halle - lu - jah!

Glo - ry! Glo-ry Hal-le-lu - jah! Glo-ry! Glory! Glory Halle - lu - jah!

Glo - ry! Glo-ry Hal-le-lu - jah! His truth is marching on.

Glo - ry! Glo-ry Hal-le-lu - jah! His truth is marching on.

Glo - ry! Glo-ry Hal-le-lu - jah! His truth is marching on.

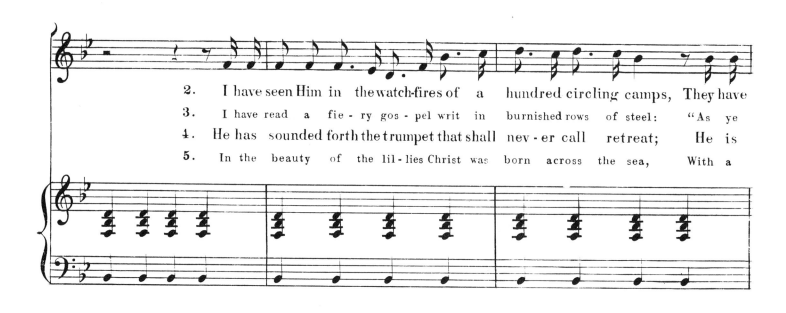

2. I have seen Him in the watch-fires of a hundred circling camps, They have
3. I have read a fie - ry gos - pel writ in burnished rows of steel: "As ye
4. He has sounded forth the trumpet that shall nev - er call retreat; He is
5. In the beauty of the lil - lies Christ was born across the sea, With a

builded Him an al - tar in the evening dews and damps; I can read His righteous sentence by the
deal with my contemners, so with you my grace shall deal; Let the He - ro born of wo - man crush the
sift - ing out the hearts of men be - fore His judgment seat: Oh, be swift, my soul, to answer Him! be
glo - ry in his bo - som that trans - fig - ures you and me: As he died to make men ho - ly, let us

**Chorus.**

dim and flaring lamps: His day is march - ing on.
ser - pent with his heel, Since God is march - ing on.
ju - bi - lant, my feet! Our God is march - ing on.
die to make men free, While God is march ing on.

**Chorus.**

The popular refrain of

# GLORY, HALLELUJAH

AS SUNG BY THE

# Federal Volunteers

Throughout the Union.

PIANO. ———————— 2½ ———————— GUITAR.

Boston
Published by Oliver Ditson & Co 277 Washington St
Firth. Pond & Co.    J. Church. Jr.    J. C. Haynes & Co.    J. E. Gould    C. C. Clapp & Co.
N. York        Cinn.        Boston        Philad?        Boston
Entered according to act of Congress A 1861 by O. Ditson & Co in the Clerks Office of the Dist Court of Mass

# GLORY! GLORY! HALLELUJAH!

4.

|: Ellsworth's (John Brown's) knapsack is strapped upon his back, :|
His soul is marching on.
         CHORUS. Glory &c.

5.

|: His pet lambs will meet him on the way, :|
And they'll go marching on.
         CHORUS.

6.

|: They will hang Jeff Davis to a tree, :|
As they march along.
         CHORUS.

7.

|: Let's give three good rousing cheers for the union. :|

As we're marching on.

CHORUS. Glory, &c.

Hip, hip, hip, hip, Hurrah!

Words dedicated to and sung by the Fourth Battalion of Rifles. 13th Regiment Massachusetts Volunteers.

1.

Cheer for the banner as we rally 'neath its stars,

As we join the Northern legion and are off for the wars,

Ready for the onset, for bullet, blood and scars!

Cheer for the dear old flag!

CHORUS. Glory! Glory! Glory for the North!

Glory to the soldiers she is sending forth!

Glory! Glory! Glory for the North!

They'll conquer as they go.

2.

Cheer for the sweethearts we are now forced to leave,

Think of us, lassies, but for us don't grieve,

Bright be the garlands that for us you'll weave,

When we return to your smiles.

CHORUS.

3.

Blank looks in Dixie when Northern troops come!

Sad hearts in Dixie when they hear the victor's drum!

Pale cheeks in Dixie when rattle, shell and bomb,

And down goes the Dixie rag!

CHORUS.

4.

Swift heels in Dixie, but swifter on their track!

We'll meet them on their stumping ground and quickly drive 'em back!

Nimble feet in Dixie when they hear the rifle's crack

Of the Old Bay States' Thirteenth!

CHORUS.

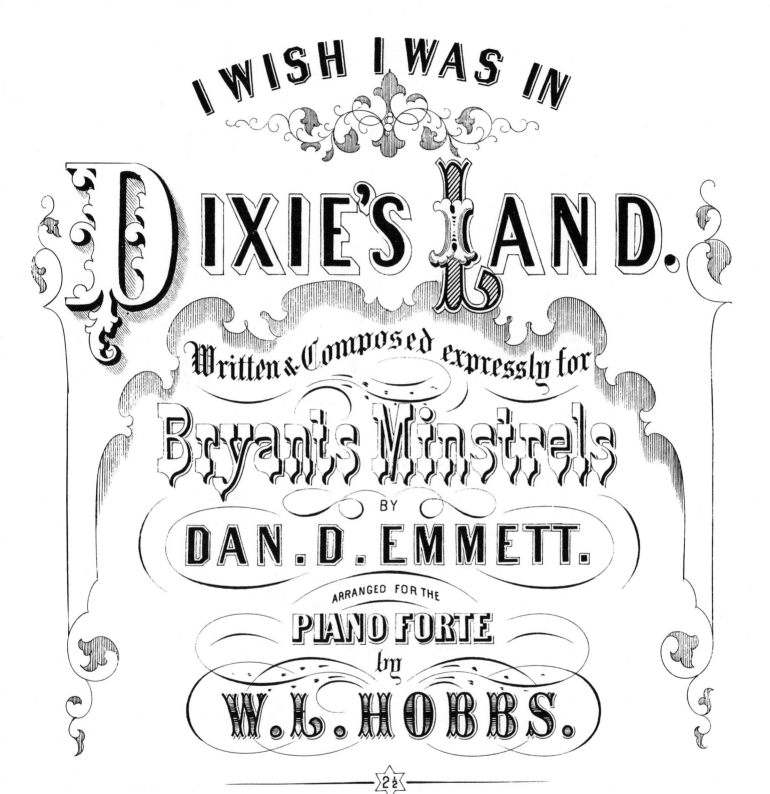

# I WISH I WAS IN

# Dixie's Land.

Written & Composed expressly for

## Bryants Minstrels

BY

## DAN. D. EMMETT.

ARRANGED FOR THE

### PIANO FORTE

by

### W. L. HOBBS.

2½

NEW YORK
Published by FIRTH, POND & CO. 547 Broadway.

Boston,
O. DITSON & CO.

Cincinnati.
C. Y. FONDA.

Pittsburgh.
H. KLEBER & BRO.

Entered according to act of Congress in the Year 1860 by Firth Pond & Co in the Clerks Office of the District Court of the South'n District of New York.

# DIXIE'S LAND

COMPOSED BY DAN' EMMETT.

ARRANGED BY W. L. HOBBS.

I wish I was in de land ob cot - ton, Old times dar am not for - got - ten; Look a - way! Look a - way! Look a - way! Dix - ie Land. In Dix - ie Land whar I was born in, Ear - ly on one fros - ty morn - in, Look a -

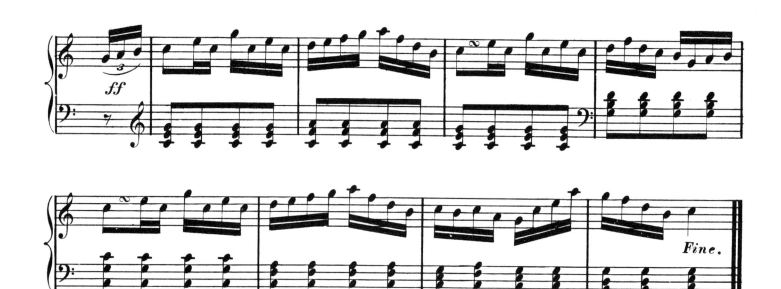

**2.**

Old Missus marry "Will-de-weaber,"
Willium was a gay deceaber;
      Look away! &c_
But when he put his arm around'er,
He smilled as fierce as a 'forty-pound'er.
      Look away! &c_
    *Chorus_* Den I wish I was in Dixie, &c_

**3.**

His face was sharp as a butchers cleaber,
But dat did not seem to greab'er;
      Look away! &c_
Old Missus acted de foolish part,
And died for a man dat broke her heart.
      Look away! &c_
    *Chorus_* Den I wish I was in Dixie, &c_

**4.**

Now here's a health to the next old Missus,
An all de galls dat want to kiss us;
      Look away! &c_
But if you want to drive'way sorrow,
Come an hear dis song to-morrow.
      Look away! &c_
    *Chorus_* Den I wish I was in Dixie, &c_

**5.**

Dar's buck-wheat cakes an 'Ingen' batter,
Makes you fat or a little fatter;
      Look away! &c_
Den hoe it down an scratch your grabble,
To Dixie land I'm bound to trabble.
      Look away! &c_
    *Chorus_* Den I wish I was in Dixie, &c_

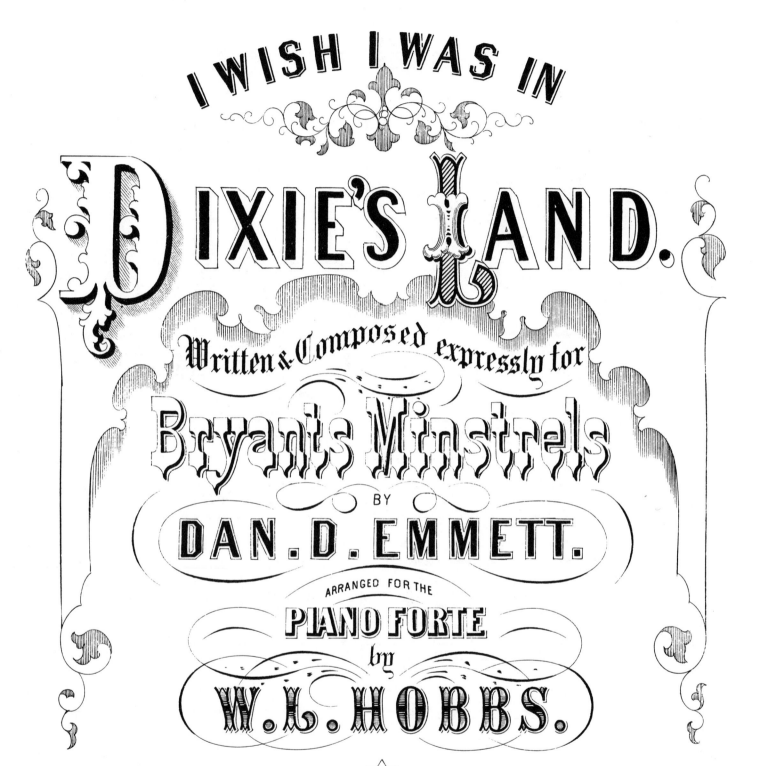

# I WISH I WAS IN
# DIXIE'S LAND.

Written & Composed expressly for

## Bryants Minstrels

BY

## DAN. D. EMMETT.

ARRANGED FOR THE

## PIANO FORTE

by

## W. L. HOBBS.

2½

NEW YORK
Published by FIRTH, POND & CO. 547 Broadway.

Boston.
O. DITSON & CO.

Cincinnati.
C. Y. FONDA.

Pittsburgh.
H. KLEBER & BRO.

# DIXIE'S LAND

Composed by DAN' EMMETT.

Arranged by W. L. HOBBS.

I wish I was in de land ob cot - ton,
Old times dar am not for - got - ten; Look a - way! Look a - way! Look a - way! Dix - ie Land. In Dix - ie Land whar I was born in, Ear - ly on one fros - ty morn - in, Look a -

Ent'd according to Act of Congress, AD 1860 by Firth, Pond & Co. in the Clerk's Office of the Dis't Court of the South'n Dis't of N.Y.

To ALBERT G. PIKE, Esq., the Poet-Lawyer of Arkansas.

# THE

# BONNIE BLUE FLAG

## A SOUTHERN PATRIOTIC SONG,

Written, Arranged, and Sung at his "Personation Concerts,"

BY

# HARRY MACARTHY,

## THE ARKANSAS COMEDIAN,

Author of "Origin of the Stars and Bars,"
"The Volunteer,"
"Missouri."

3

## NEW ORLEANS:

Published by A. E. BLACKMAR & BRO., 74 Camp Street.

| COLUMBIA, S. C., | PETERSBURG, VA., | WILMINGTON, N. C., | HUNTSVILLE, ALA., |
|---|---|---|---|
| TOWNSEND & NORTH. | J. E. ROUTH. | T. S. WHITAKER. | LOGEMAN & HOLLENBERG. |

Entered according to act of Congress, A. D. 1861, by Harry Macarthy, in the District Court of the C. S. for the District of Louisiana.

# THE BONNIE BLUE FLAG

HARRY MACARTHY.

With Spirit.

PIANO.

We are a band of brothers, And na_tive to the soil, Fighting for our Lib_er_ty, With treasure,blood and toil; And when our rights were threaten'd, The cry rose near and far, Hur_

_ rah      for      the      Bon_nie Blue Flag, that   bears   a   Sin_gle      Star!

CHORUS.

Hur _ rah !      Hur _ rah !      for  Southern Rights Hur_rah !      Hur_rah! for the

Bon_nie Blue Flag that bears a Sin_gle      Star!

As long as the Union was faithful to her trust, Like friends and like

bretheren kind were we and just; But now when Northern treache_ry at_

_tempts our rights to mar, We hoist on high the Bonnie Blue Flag that bears a Single Star.

CHORUS. Hurrah! &c

### 3rd V.

First, gallant South Carolina nobly made the stand;
Then came Alabama, who took her by the hand;
Next, quickly Mississippi, Georgia and Florida,
All rais'd on high the Bonnie Blue Flag that bears a Single Star.

CHORUS. Hurrah! &c.

### 4th V.

Ye men of valor, gather round the Banner of the Right,
Texas and fair Louisiana, join us in the fight;
Davis, our loved President, and Stephens, Stateman rare,
Now rally round the Bonnie Blue Flag that bears a Single Star.

CHORUS. Hurrah! &c.

### 5th V.

And here's to brave Virginia! the Old Dominion State
With the young Confederacy at length has link'd her fate;
Impell'd by her example, now other State prepare
To hoist on high the Bonnie Blue Flag that bears a Single Star.

CHORUS. Hurrah! &c.

### 6th V.

Then cheer, boys, raise the joyous shout,
For Arkansas and North Carolina now have both gone out;
And let another rousing cheer for Tennessee be given
The Single Star of the Bonnie Blue Flag has grown to be Eleven.

CHORUS. Hurrah! &c.

### 7th V.

Then here's to our Confederacy, strong we are and brave,
Like patriots of old, we'll fight our heritage to save;
And rather than submit to shame, to die we would prefer,
So cheer for the Bonnie Blue Flag that bears a Single Star.


### CHORUS.

Hurrah! Hurrah! for Southern Rights, hurrah!
Hurrah! for the Bonnie Blue Flag has gain'd th' Eleventh Star!

Wehrmann Engr N.O.

# MARYLAND! MY MARYLAND.

### Crescite et Multiplicamini,

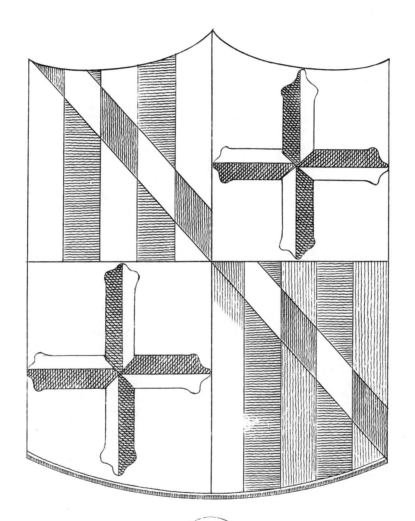

Written by

## A Baltimorean in Louisianna

Music Adapted & Arranged by

## C. E.

Published by MILLER & BEACHAM Baltimore.

Entered according to Act of Congress AD 1861 by Miller & Beacham in the Clerks Office of the District Court of Md.

# MARYLAND, MY MARYLAND!

### 3

Thou wilt not cower in the dust,
    Maryland! My Maryland!
Thy beaming sword shall never rust,
    Maryland! My Maryland!
Remember Carroll's sacred trust,
Remember Howard's warlike thrust—
And all thy slumberers with the just,
    Maryland! My Maryland!

### 4

Come! for thy shield is bright and strong,
    Maryland! My Maryland!
Come! for thy dalliance, does thee wrong,
    Maryland! My Maryland!
Come! to thine own heroic throng,
That stalks with Liberty along,
And give a new Key to thy song,
    Maryland! My Maryland!

### 5

Dear Mother! burst the tyrant's chain,
    Maryland! My Maryland!
Virginia should not call in vain!
    Maryland! My Maryland!
She meets her sisters on the plain—
"Sic semper" tis the proud refrain,
That baffles minions back amain,
    Maryland! My Maryland!

### 6

I see the blush upon thy cheek,
    Maryland! My Maryland!
But thou wast ever bravely meek,
    Maryland! My Maryland!
But lo! there surges forth a shriek
From hill to hill, from creek to creek—
Potomac calls to Chesapeake,
    Maryland! My Maryland!

### 7

Thou wilt not yield the vandal toll,
    Maryland! My Maryland!
Thou wilt not crook to his control,
    Maryland! My Maryland!
Better the fire upon thee roll,
Better the blade, the shot, the bowl,
Than crucifixion of the soul,
    Maryland! My Maryland!

### 8

I hear the distant thunder-hum,
    Maryland! My Maryland!
The Old Line's bugle, fife and drum,
    Maryland! My Maryland!
She is not dead, nor deaf, nor dumb—
Huzza! she spurns the Northern scum!
She breathes— she burns! she'll come! she'll come!
    Maryland! My Maryland!

# The Southrons

## CHAUNT of DEFIANCE

*"You can never win us back
Never! Never!
Though we perish on the track
Of your endeavor"*

### Song or Quartette

Written by a Lady of Kentucky.

Music by

## A. E. Blackmar.

AUTHOR OF "GOD & OUR RIGHTS."

W.L. Tetson N.O.

3½

NEW ORLEANS.
Published by A.E. BLACKMAR & BRO. 74. Camp St

| Charleston. | Mobile. | Memphis. | Baton Rouge. |
|---|---|---|---|
| H. SIEGLING. | J H. SNOW. | JAS. A. McCLURE. | E & W. BOGEL. |
| GEO. F. COLE. | BROMBERG & SON. | E A. BENSON. | GEO. HERDMAN. |

Entered according to Act of Congress AD 1864 by BLACKMAR & Co in the Clerk's Off. of the Dist. Court of the East. Dist. of La

# Southrons' CHAUNT of DEFIANCE

### BY A. E. Blackmar.

PIANO.

V. 1. You can nev _ er win us back; Nev _ er! Nev _ er!
V. 2. We have ris _ _ en to a man, Stern and fear _ less;

Tho' we per _ ish in the track of your en _ _ deavor;
Of your cur _ ses, of your ban, We are care _ less.

You have no such blood as ours
   For the shedding;
In the veins of Cavaliers
   Was its heading!
You have no such stately men
In your abolition den
Marching on through foe and fen,
   Nothing dreading!

We may fall before the fire
   Of your legions,
Paid with gold for murderous hire,
   Bought allegiance;
But for every drop you shed,
You shall have a mound of dead,
So that vultures may be fed
   In our regions!

But the battle to the strong
   Is not given,
While the Judge of right and wrong
   Sits in Heaven
And the God of David still
Guides the pebble with His will,
There are giants yet to kill,
   Wrongs unshriven!

# CHANT OF DEFIANCE.

### QUARTETTE.

SOPRANO. You can nev_er win us back; Nev_er! nev_er!

ALTO. We have ris_en to a man; Stern and fearless!

TENOR. We may fall be _ fore the fire Of your legions,

BASS. But the bat_tle to the strong Is not giv_en,

Tho' we per_ish in the track Of your en _ deav_or;

Of your cur_ses, of your ban, We are care_less,

Paid with gold for mur d'rous hire, Bought al _ _ legiance;

While the Judge of Right and Wrong Sits in Heav_en.

# We are coming Father Abra'am

# 300,000

## MORE

### POETRY BY
# Wm. Cullen Bryant,

### Music by
# L. O. EMERSON.

Boston.
Published by Oliver Ditson & Co. 277 Washington St.

Firth Pond & Co.      J Church Jr.      J.C. Haynes & Co.      J.E. Gould.      G.C. Clapp & Co.
N. York.              Cin.              Boston.                Philad?           Boston.

# WE ARE COMING FATHER ABRA'AM.

L. O. Emerson.

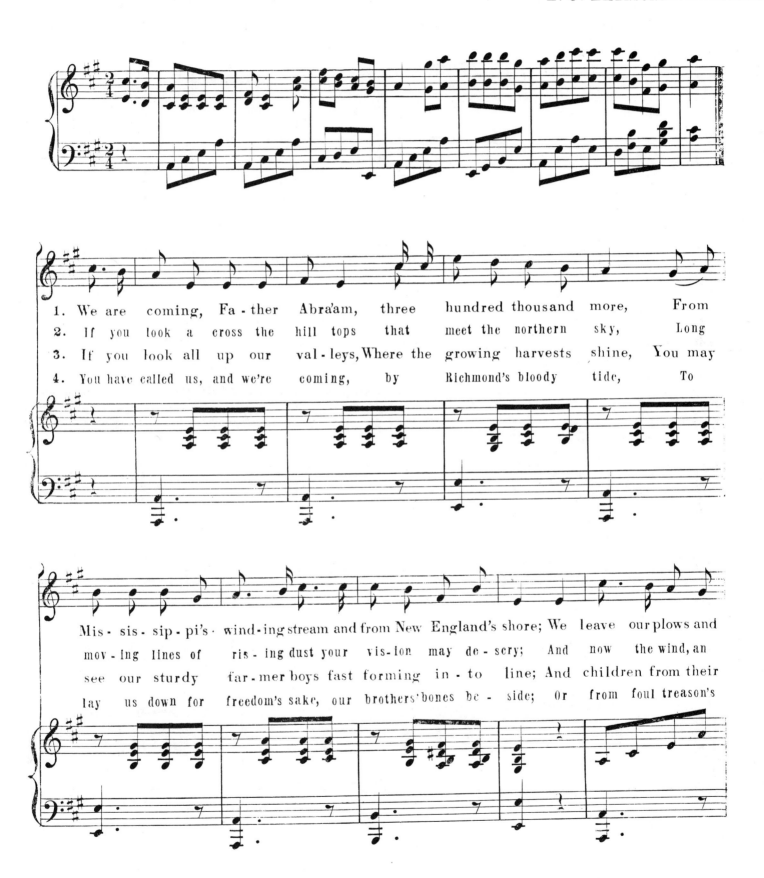

1. We are coming, Fa-ther Abra'am, three hundred thousand more, From
2. If you look a-cross the hill tops that meet the northern sky, Long
3. If you look all up our val-leys, Where the growing harvests shine, You may
4. You have called us, and we're coming, by Richmond's bloody tide, To

Mis-sis-sip-pi's wind-ing stream and from New England's shore; We leave our plows and
mov-ing lines of ris-ing dust your vis-ion may de-scry; And now the wind, an
see our sturdy far-mer boys fast forming in-to line; And children from their
lay us down for freedom's sake, our brothers' bones be-side; Or from foul treason's

workshops our wives and children dear, With hearts too full for ut - terance, with
in - stant, tears the cloudy veil a - - side, And floats aloft our spangled flag in
mother's knees are pulling at the weeds, And learning how to reap and sow, a -
savage group, to wrench the murderous blade, And in the face of fo - reign foes its

but a si - lent tear; We dare not look be - hind us, but steadfastly be -
glo - ry and in pride; And bayonets in the sunlight gleam, and bands brave mu - sic
gainst their country's needs; And a farewell group stands weep - ing at every cot - tage
frag - ments to pa - rade; Six hundred thousand loy-al men and true have gone be -

fore _
pour _
door _     We are coming, Father Abra'am _ three hundred thousand more!
fore _

## Chorus

We are coming, we are coming, Our U-nion to re-store; We are coming, Father

Abra'am with three hundred thousand more, We are coming Father Abra'am With three hundred thousand more.

Abra'am With three hundred thousand more, We are coming Father Abra'am With three hundred thousand more.

To Cousin Mary Lizzie Work,        Of New Washington, Indiana.

# MARCHING THROUGH GEORGIA

## SONG AND CHORUS,

In Honor of Maj. Gen. SHERMAN'S FAMOUS MARCH "from Atlanta to the Sea."

Words and Music by

# HENRY CLAY WORK.

## CHICAGO:

### PUBLISHED BY ROOT & CADY. 67 WASHINGTON ST.

# MARCHING THROUGH GEORGIA.

Words and Music by HENRY C. WORK.

1. Bring the good old bu - gle, boys! we'll
2. How the dar - keys shout - ed when they
3. Yes, and there were Un - ion men who
4. "Sher - man's dash - ing Yan - kee boys will
5. So we made a thor - ough - fare for

sing an - oth - er song— Sing it with a spir - it that will
heard the joy - ful sound! How the tur - keys gob - bled which our
wept with joy - ful tears, When they saw the hon - or'd flag they
nev - er reach the coast!" So the sau - cy reb - els said, and
Free - dom and her train, Six - ty miles in la - ti - tude— three

start the world a - long— Sing it as we used to sing it,
com - mis - sa - ry found! How the sweet po - ta - toes e - ven
had not seen for years; Hard - ly could they be re - strained from
'twas a hand - some boast, Had they not for - got, a - las! to
hun - dred to the main; Trea - son fled be - fore us, for re-

fif - ty thou - sand strong, While we were march - ing through Geor - gia.
start - ed from the ground, While we were march - ing through Geor - gia.
break - ing forth in cheers, While we were march - ing through Geor - gia.
reck - on with the host, While we were march - ing through Geor - gia.
sis - tance was in vain, While we were march - ing through Geor - gia.

CHORUS.

Air.
"Hur - rah! Hur - rah! we bring the Ju - bi - lee! Hur - rah! Hur - rah! the

Alto. ff

Tenor.
"Hur - rah! Hur - rah! we bring the Ju - bi - lee! Hur - rah! Hur - rah! tho

Base. ff

flag that makes you free!" So we sang the cho - rus from At-

flag that makes you free!" So we sang the cho - rus from At-

lan - ta to the sea, While we were march - ing through Geor - gia.

lan - ta to the sea, While we were march - ing through Geor - gia.

TO PERPETUATE
the glory of the brave men of the
➤ 19th Illinois, ◄
and their companions in arms who fell at
MURFREESBORO.

# "Who'll save the left,"

## A Battle Scene.

WORDS BY

# R. Tompkins,

MUSIC BY

# GEO. F. ROOT.

CHICAGO.

Published by ROOT & CADY 95 Clark St.

# "WHO'LL SAVE THE LEFT?"

R.T. & G.F.R.

Recitando

Thro' two long days the battle raged In front of Mur-frees-bo-ro    And

tremolo

can-non balls tore up the earth As plows turn up the furrow    Brave soldiers by the hundred fell    In

fierce assault and sally    While bursting shell hiss'd scream'd and fell Like demons in the val-ley    The

Northman, and the Southron met, In bold de-fi-ant man-ner, Now vic-t'ry perch'd on Un-ion flag, And

now on rebel banner; But see! upon the Un-ion's left, Bear down in countless numbers, With

shouts that seem to wake the hills From their e-ter-nal slum-bers, The reb-el hosts, whose i-ron rain Beats

down our weaker forces, And cov-ers all the battle plain With torn and mangled corses; Still

onward press the rebel hordes More boldly, fiercer, faster,      But Neg-ley's practiced eye discerns The

swift and dread disaster, "Who'll save the left," his voice rang out A-bove the roar of battle,      "The

Nineteenth" shouted Colonel Scott, Amid the muskets rattle      "The Nineteenth be it,    Make the charge!"

Quick as the word was given,  The Nineteenth fell up on the foe, As  lightning   falls from heaven.

7

TRAMP! TRAMP! TRAMP! or the PRISONER'S HOPE.

AS SUNG BY EDWIN KELLEY,

OF ARLINGTON KELLEY & LEON'S MINSTRELS.

Song & Chorus.

BY GEO. F. ROOT.

Published by Root & Cady.

67 Washington St.

CHICAGO.

# TRAMP! TRAMP! TRAMP!

## ( THE PRISONER'S HOPE.)

*Tempo di Marcia.*

Words and Music By GEO. F. ROOT.

1. In the pris - on cell I sit, Think-ing Moth - er dear, of you, And our bright and hap - py home so far a - way, And the tears they fill my eyes Spite of

2. In the bat - tle front we stood When their fierc - est charge they made, And they swept us off a hun-dred men or more, But be - fore we reach'd their lines They were

3. So with - in the pris - on cell, We are wait - ing for the day That shall come to o - pen wide the i - ron door, And the hol - low eye grows bright, And the

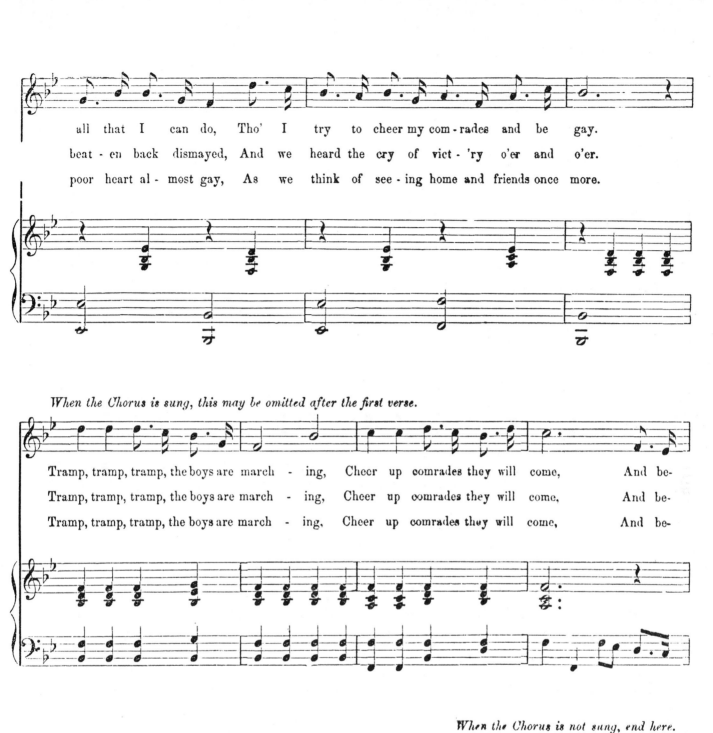

all that I can do, Tho' I try to cheer my com-rades and be gay.

beat-en back dismayed, And we heard the cry of vict-'ry o'er and o'er.

poor heart al-most gay, As we think of see-ing home and friends once more.

*When the Chorus is sung, this may be omitted after the first verse.*

Tramp, tramp, tramp, the boys are march - ing, Cheer up comrades they will come, And be-

Tramp, tramp, tramp, the boys are march - ing, Cheer up comrades they will come, And be-

Tramp, tramp, tramp, the boys are march - ing, Cheer up comrades they will come, And be-

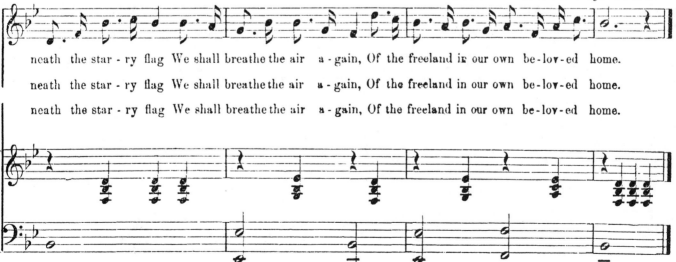

*When the Chorus is not sung, end here.*

neath the star - ry flag We shall breathe the air a - gain, Of the freeland in our own be-lov-ed home.

neath the star - ry flag We shall breathe the air a - gain, Of the freeland in our own be-lov-ed home.

neath the star - ry flag We shall breathe the air a - gain, Of the freeland in our own be-lov-ed home.

## CHORUS.

Tramp, tramp, tramp, the boys are march - ing, Cheer up comrades they will come. And be-neath the star - ry flag We shall breathe the air a - gain, Of the free-land in our own be-lov-ed home.

Tramp, tramp, tramp, the boys are march-ing on, O cheer up com - rades they will come, And be-neath the star - ry flag We shall breathe the air a - gain, Of the free-land in our own be-lov-ed home.

Tramp, tramp, tramp, the boys are march-ing, on, O cheer up com - rades . they will come, And be-neath the star - ry flag We shall breathe the air a - gain, Of the free-land in our own be-lov-ed home.

# Just before the battle, MOTHER.

Song & Chorus

by

GEO. F. ROOT.

Published by ROOT & CADY 95 Clark St.

CHICAGO.

# JUST BEFORE THE BATTLE, MOTHER.

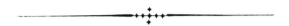

Words & Music by GEO. F. ROOT.

1. Just be-fore the bat-tle, Moth-er,  I  am thinking most of  you;
2. Oh,  I  long to  see you, Moth-er;  And the lov-ing ones at  home;
3. Hark! I  hear the bu-gles sounding,  Tis  the sig-nal for the  fight,

While up - on the field we're watching, With the en- -e- -my in view.
But, I'll nev - er leave our banner, Till in hon or I can come.
Now may God pro - tect us, Mother, As He ev - -er does the right.

Comrades brave are round me ly - ing, Fill'd with tho'ts of home and God; For
Tell the traitors, all a - round you, That their cru - el words, we know, In
✻ Hear the "Bat - tle - Cry of Free - dom", How it swells up - on the air; Oh,

well they know, that on the morrow, Some will sleep be - neath the sod.
ev' - ry bat - tle kill our sol - diers By the help they give the foe.
yes we'll ral - ly round the standard, Or we'll per - ish no - bly there.

✻ In the Army of the Cumberland, the Soldiers sing the Battle-Cry when going into action, by order of the Commanding General.

CHORUS

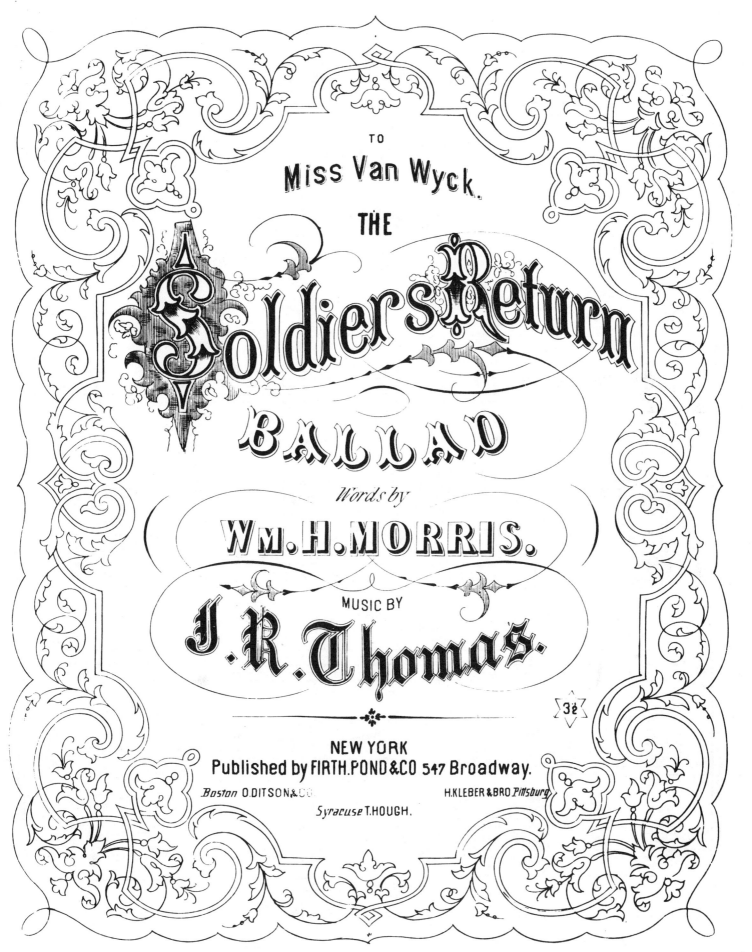

# THE
# SOLDIER'S RETURN.

### *BALLAD.*

Words by
### W. H. MORRIS.

Music by
### J. R. THOMAS.

**Allegretto.**

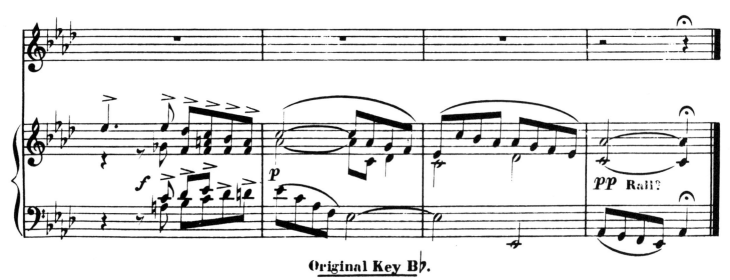

**Original Key B♭.**

well    I know she will be - stow .......... The same    when I    re-

-turn! .... For    well    I know she will bestow ....... The same    when I re-

First time.    Second.

-turn!

(II.) When

Clayton.

# Tenting on the Old Camp Ground

WORDS & MUSIC BY

## WALTER KITTREDGE,

Adapted & sung by the

## HUTCHINSON FAMILY.

"TRIBE OF ASA."

BOSTON.
Published by Oliver Ditson & Co 277 Washington St.

Cinn.          N.York.          Boston.          Ph.a
J.Church Jr    W.A.Pond & Co.   J.C.Haynes & Co.  J.E.Gould

Entered according to act of Congress AD 1864 by O. Ditson & Co. in the Clerk's office of the Dist Court of Mass.

# TENTING ON THE OLD CAMP GROUND.

Arranged by M.F.H. SMITH.

1 We're tent-ing to-night on the old Camp ground, Give us a song to cheer Our
2 We've been tent-ing to-night on the old Camp ground, Thinking of days gone by, Of the
3 We are tired of war on the old Camp ground, Many are dead and gone, Of the
4 We've been fight-ing to-day on the old Camp ground, Many are ly-ing near;

weary hearts, a song of home, And friends we love so dear.
lov'd ones at home that gave us the hand, And the tear that said, "Good bye!
brave and true who've left their homes, Others been wounded long.
Some are dead and some are dying, Many are in tears.

CHORUS.

Many are the hearts that are weary to-night, Wishing for the war to

# ALL QUIET

## ALONG THE

## POTOMAC

## TO-NIGHT.

BALTIMORE:

3.

Published by MILLER & BEACHAM, No. 10 North Charles Street.

# "ALL QUIET ALONG THE POTOMAC TO-NIGHT."

MODERATO.

"All qui - et a - long the Po - to - mac to-night," Ex - cept here and there a stray picket Is

shot as he walks on his beat to and fro, By a ri - fleman hid in the thicket; 'Tis

noth-ing! a pri-vate or two now and then, Will not count in the news of the bat-tle, Not an

of-fi-cer lost! on-ly one of the men Moaning out all a-lone the death rattle. "All

qui - et a - long...... the Po-to - mac to - night!"

## 2

"All quiet along the Potomac to-night,"
    Where the soldiers lie peacefully dreaming,
And their tents in the rays of the clear autumn moon,
    And the light of the camp fires are gleaming;
There's only the sound of the lone sentry's tread,
    As he tramps from the rock to the fountain,
And thinks of the two on the low trundle bed
    Far away in the cot on the mountain.

## 3

His musket falls slack — his face, dark and grim,
    Grows gentle with memories tender,
As he mutters a pray'r for the children asleep,
    And their mother — "May heaven defend her!"
The moon seems to shine as brightly as then —
    That night, when the love yet unspoken
Leap'd up to his lips, and when low murmur'd vows
    Were pledg'd, to be ever unbroken.

## 4

Then drawing his sleeve roughly o'er his eyes,
    He dashes off the tears that are welling,
And gathers his gun close up to his breast,
    As if to keep down the heart's swelling;
He passes the fountain, the blasted pine tree,
    And his footstep is lagging and weary,
Yet onward he goes, thro' the broad belt of light,
    Toward the shades of the forest so dreary.

## 5

Hark! was it the night-wind that rustles the leaves!
    Was it the moonlight so wond'rously flashing?
It look'd like a rifle! "Ha, Mary good bye!"
    And his life-blood is ebbing and plashing.
"All quiet along the Potomac to-night,"
    No sound save the rush of the river;
While soft falls the dew on the face of the dead,
    "The Picket's" off duty for ever.

Clayton

TO
"OUR DELUDED BRETHERN"

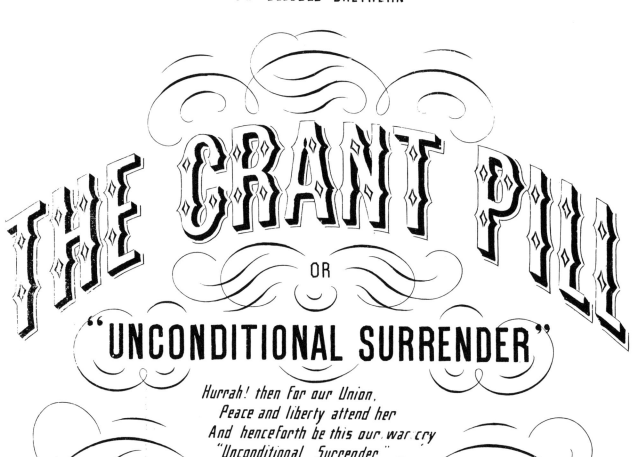

# THE GRANT PILL

OR

## "UNCONDITIONAL SURRENDER"

*Hurrah! then for our Union,*
*Peace and liberty attend her*
*And henceforth be this our war cry*
*"Unconditional Surrender"*

WORDS BY

### HARRIET L. CASTLE

Music Arranged by

### J. C. BECKEL.

Philadelphia
Published by W. R. SMITH Agt 135 N.th Eighth St.

# THE GRANT PILL

## J. C. BECKEL.

Allegro moderato.

PIANO.

1. You   see my jol-ly comrades We are ripe and prime for battle   We
3. "Tis   un-chi-valric treatment To a   man in my   condition But

heeded not the cannon's roar nor grape shot's hissing rattle We were sworn to Death or victory for our
I yield me" said their leader so our armies gain'd admission Then our Flag went up instanter as she

cres.

f

Un - ion God defend her And to on-ly take from Re-bels uncon ditional surrender,
must, when braves defend her And while leaders have this warcry "Unconditional surrender."

un-condition - al, un - con - di - tional, un - con - di - tion - al surrender.

2. A - 'midst the din of warfare and the shrieks of hosts a - dy-ing We
4. Hur-rah! then for our Union Our Flag and Con - sti - tu-tion, While we've

# O, I'M A GOOD OLD REBEL

# O I'm a Good Old Rebel.

### A Chaunt to the Wild Western Melody, "Joe Bowers."

## RESPECTFULLY DEDICATED TO THE HON. THAD. STEVENS.

O I'm a good old reb----el, Now that's just what I am, For this "Fair Land of Free----dom" I do not care AT ALL; I'm glad I fit a----gainst it— I on---ly wish we'd

won    And    I    don't want    no    par----don    For    an---y    thing    I    done.

I hates the Constitution,
　　This Great Republic, too,
I hates the Freedman's Buro,
　　In uniforms of blue;
I hates the nasty eagle,
　　With all his braggs and fuss,
The lyin', thievin' Yankees,
　　I hates 'em wuss and wuss.

I hates the Yankee nation
　　And everything they do,
I hates the Declaration
　　Of Independence, too;
I hates the glorious Union—
　　'Tis dripping with our blood—
I hates their striped banner,
　　I fit it all I could.

I followed old mas' Robert
　　For four year, near about,
Got wounded in three places
　　And starved at Pint Lookout;
I cotch the roomatism
　　A campin' in the snow,
But I killed a chance o' Yankees,
　　I'd like to kill some mo'.

Three hundred thousand Yankees
　　Is stiff in Southern dust;
We GOT three hundred thousand
　　Before they conquered us;
They died of Southern fever
　　And Southern steel and shot,
I wish they was three million
　　Instead of what we got.

I can't take up my musket
　　And fight 'em now no more,
But I aint a going to love 'em,
　　Now that is sarten sure;
And I don't want no pardon
　　For what I was and am,
I won't be reconstructed
　　And I don't care a dam.

# THE CHILDREN
## OF THE
# BATTLE FIELD.

## POETRY AND MUSIC
### BY
# JAMES G. CLARK
### RESPECTFULLY DEDICATED TO
# J. FRANCIS BOURNS, M.D.
#### OF PHILADELPHIA, PA.

*honored for his living patriotism and philanthropy,*
*this song is most cordially and respectfully dedicated by*
——— ❖ ———                    *THE AUTHOR.*

Philadelphia LEE & WALKER 722 Chestnut St.

T. SINCLAIR'S LITH, PHILA,

# SKETCH.

FEW readers of the public journals will fail to remember that, after the battle of Gettysburg, a dead soldier was found on the field, clasping in his hand an ambrotype of his three little children. No other incident of the present fratricidal war is known to have so touched the heart of the nation. For months after the battle, the soldier's name, and the home of his family, were a mystery. The ambrotype found within his clasped hands was obtained by J. FRANCIS BOURNS, M.D., of Philadelphia, who had the picture photographed, in the hope that its circulation might lead to the discovery of the family, and the soldier's own recognition, and, at the same time, that the sales of the copies might result in a fund for the support and education of the little ones thus left fatherless. Publicity was also given to the incident in many newspapers throughout the country. From various quarters letters of affecting inquiry were soon received; but still the mystery of the soldier was unsolved. At length, in the month of November, a letter arrived with the intelligence that a soldier's wife at a little town on the Allegheny River, in Western New York, had seen the account of the picture in a religious paper, the *American Presbyterian*, of Philadelphia,—a single copy of which was taken in the place. She had sent her husband such a picture, and had not heard from him since the sanguinary struggle at Gettysburg. With trembling anxiety she awaited the reply and the coming of the picture. A copy of it came, and was the identical likeness of her own children, and told the painful story that she was a widow and her little ones were orphans. The unknown soldier was thus ascertained to be AMOS HUMISTON, late of Portville, Cattaraugus county, New York, sergeant in the 154th N.Y. Volunteers.

Rev. ISAAC G. OGDEN, pastor of the Presbyterian church at Portville, wrote respecting the deceased, that " he was a man of noble impulses, a quiet citizen, a kind neighbor, and devotedly attached to his family. When the rebellion first took the form of open war upon the country, he was anxious to enlist; but his duty to his family seemed then to be paramount to his duty to his country. But after the disastrous Peninsular campaign, when there was a call for three hundred thousand more volunteers, and when he received assurance from responsible citizens that his family should be cared for during his absence, then, without the prospect of a large bounty, he enlisted as a private in the 154th N.Y. State Volunteers. He was with his regiment in the battle of Chancellorsville, and was promoted to the office of orderly sergeant. At Gettysburg he fought with great gallantry, and on its bloody field laid down his life for his country."

His children—FRANK, FREDERICK, and ALICE—are bright, active, and intelligent, and, with their widowed mother, are left a legacy to the country for which their patriot-father died. It was certainly a remarkable providence which made Sergeant HUMISTON's attachment to his children the means of his recognition, and likewise the means of awakening so lively an interest in his bereaved family, if not also in many families similarly stricken and cast upon the country.

The fine lithograph on the title-page is an accurate copy of the original picture which was found in the hands of the dead hero, and a correct likeness of his children. The following simple, sweet verses originally appeared in the religious paper referred to above, having received the premium awarded for a poem on the subject by the publisher. The music, as well as the song, is from the same gifted author.

---

## COMMENDATION FROM THE REV. JOHN W. MEARS.

PHILADELPHIA, March 23, 1864.

In view of the very humane and worthy object contemplated in this publication, and in the hope that its wide circulation may stimulate patriotism and help to keep alive in the national heart a sense of our unspeakable indebtedness to the families who have been reduced to dependence by the heroic devotion and martyrdom of fathers, husbands, and sons, in the service of our common country, I cheerfully give my testimony to the correctness of the foregoing statement, and commend the " Children of the Battle-Field" to the patronage of the loyal people.

JOHN W. MEARS,
Editor of the *American Presbyterian*.

No. 1334 Chestnut Street.

---

☞ *The net proceeds of the sales of this Music are reserved for the support and education of the Orphan Children.*

# THE CHILDREN
## OF THE BATTLE FIELD.

POETRY & MUSIC       —       BY J.G.CLARK.

AS SUNG BY THE AUTHOR, AT HIS BALLAD ENTERTAINMENTS.

Up _ on the field of Gettys_burg The

summer sun was high, When freedom met her haughty foe, Beneath a northern sky; A

**FATHER**, shield the soldier's wife, And for his children care, And for his chil-dren care.

## 3

Upon the field of Gettysburg
    When morning shone again,
The crimson cloud of battle burst
    In streams of fiery rain;
Our legions quelled the awful flood
    Of shot, and steel, and shell,
While banners, marked with ball and blood,
    Around them rose and fell;
And none more nobly won the name
    Of Champion of the Free,
Than he who pressed the little frame
    That held his children three;
And none were braver in the strife
    Than he who breathed the prayer:
O! **FATHER**, shield the soldier's wife,
    And for his children care.

Upon the Field of Gettysburg
    The full moon slowly rose,
She looked, and saw ten thousand brows
    All pale in death's repose,
And down beside a silver stream,
    From other forms away,
Calm as a warrior in a dream,
    Our fallen comrade lay;
His limbs were cold, his sightless eyes
    Were fixed upon the three
Sweet stars that rose in mem'ry's skies
    To light him o'er death's sea.
Then honored be the soldier's life,
    And hallowed be his prayer,
O! **FATHER**, shield the soldier's wife,
    And for his children care.

# Comrades, I am dying

Song & Chorus

Words by

## THOMAS MANAHAN,

MUSIC BY

## B. SONTAG.

BOSTON.

Published by Henry Tolman & Co. 291 Washington St.

Chicago.
Root & Cady.

Albany,
W. F. Sherwin.

Quebec.
A. Morgan

Entered according to act of Congress AD 1864 by H. Tolman & Co, in the Clerk's office of the Dist. Court of Mass.

# COMRADES, I AM DYING!

B. SONTAG.

Moderato.

PIANO.

1. Comrades, comrades, I am dy _ _ ing! See the crim _ son foun _ tain
2. Comrades, comrades, I am dy _ _ ing! For I see my moth _ er
3. Comrades, comrades, I am dy _ _ ing! Soon I'll be a _ mong the

flow! Sick and woun _ ded, I am dy _ _ ing On the
now: See her com _ ing down from heav _ en With a
blessed. Fare _ oh! fare you well for ev _ _ er, I am

cresc.

field a—mong the foe. But the an—gels hov-er
wreath up—on her brow. God has sent her to the
go————ing there to rest. For my mother's arms en—

round me. They will guard me while I sleep; Com—rades,
sol—dier, She will teach him how to die; And, when
—twine me, And I can no lon——ger stay; On—ward,

on—ward to the bat—tle, Do not for the sol——dier weep.
He has called my spir—it She will bear it to the sky.
comrades, to the bat—tle, An—gels they will lead the way.

TO MISS ANNIE CANNON.
LOUISVILLE, KY.

# THE DRUMMER BOY OF SHILOH.

A BEAUTIFUL BALLAD

WRITTEN & COMPOSED BY

## WILL. S. HAYS

AUTHOR OF "I'M LOOKING FOR HIM HOME &c. &c."

LOUISVILLE, KY.
Published by D. P. FAULDS 223 Main Street.

CHICAGO, ILL
ROOT & CADY.

# THE DRUMMER BOY.

by
WILL. S. HAYS.

On Shi-loh's dark and bloody ground, The dead and wounded lay; A-

mongst them was a drummer boy, Who beat the drum that day. A

wounded soldier held him up — His drum was by his side; He

clasp'd his hands, then rais'd his eyes, And prayed before he died. He

clasp'd his hands, then rais'd his eyes, And prayed before he died.

2. Look down upon the battle

field, Oh, Thou our Heavenly Friend! Have mer _ cy on our sinful

### 3

"Oh, Mother," said the dying boy,
  "Look down from heaven on me,
Receive me to thy fond embrace —
  Oh, take me home to thee.
I've loved my country as my God;
  To serve them both I've tried,"
‖:He smiled, shook hands — death seiezd the boy
  Who prayed before he died. :‖

### 4

Each soldier wept, then, like a child —
  Stout hearts were they, and brave;
The flag his winding — sheet — God's Book
  The key unto his grave.
They wrote upon a simple board
  These words;   This is a guide
‖:To those who'd mourn the drummer boy
  Who prayed before he died. :‖

### 5

Ye angels 'round the Throne of Grace,
  Look down upon the braves,
Who fought and died on Shiloh's plain,
  Now slumb'ring in their graves!
How many homes made desolate —
  How many hearts have sighed —
‖:How many, like that drummer boy,
  Who prayed before they died! :‖

J. Siinglandt. Engr. & Pr.

Dedicated to MISS LUCY A. PARKER, Greenwich Village, Mass.

# LITTLE MAJOR

## SONG OR DUETT, WITH CHORUS.

They called him "Little Major,"
The noble drummer boy;
The pride of all his regiment,
And his commander's joy.

## WORDS AND MUSIC BY

# HENRY C. WORK,

**Author of "Kingdom Coming," "Grafted into the Army," etc.**

No. 17.  — 8 —

## CLEVELAND:

Published by **S. B**RAINARD'S **S**ONS, 203 -Superior St.

Entered according to act of Congress, in the year of 1862, by Root & Cady, in the Clerk's Office of the District
Court for the Northern District of Illinois.

# LITTLE MAJOR.

Words and Music by HENRY C. WORK.
No. 17.

1. At his
2. There are

3. Now the
4. See! the

post,     the "Lit-tle Ma - jor" Dropp'd his drum,     that bat-tle day;     On the
none     to     hear or help him— All his friends     were ear-ly fled,     Save the

lights     are flash-ing round him,     And he hears     a     loy-al word,     Strangers
moon     that shone a-bove him,     Veils her face,     as     if     in grief;     And the

# THE

# DYING VOLUNTEER

of the

## 6TH MASSACHUSETTS REGIMENT,

# SONG

Compos'd & Dedicated to the

## Volunteers of the 6th Massachusetts Regt.

BY

# G. Gumpert

*( Author of Our Country's Flag. )*

Philadelphia, G. André & Co. 1104 Chesnut St.

Boston, OLIVER DITSON & CO.     Washington, W. G. METZEROTT.     RUSSELL & TOLMAN, Boston.

The Father of this dying volunteer fell in the Battle for his
country, the Son followed his footsteps, leaving his wife and
only child, to defend his Country's flag: he was killed at the riot
in Baltimore, April the 19th 1861. The last words he breathed were
"All hail to the Stars and Stripes"!!!

# THE DYING VOLUNTEER

## OF THE 6TH MASSACHUSSETTS REGT

The Poetry and Music
by G. GUMPERT.

Arranged for the Piano
by F. LOSSÉ.

1. Farewell my child, Farewell my wife, The bu-gle sound I hear;   It
3. He was the first, whose blood was spill'd, By trai-tors' hands he died;   His

calls me to the bloody strife, It calls the vo-lun-teer.   It
coun-try's love his bo-som fill'd, And dy-ing still he cried;   His

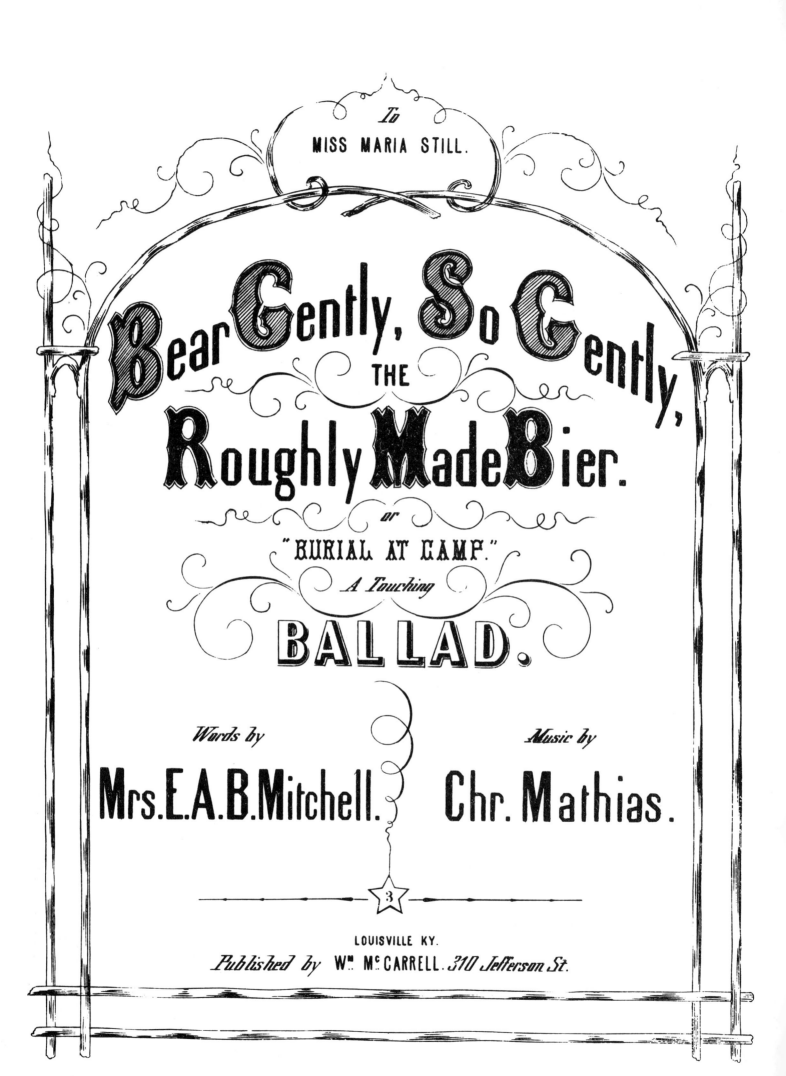

# BEAR GENTLY, SO GENTLY,

Words by Mrs. E. A. B. Mitchell.

Music by Chr. Mathias.

1. Bear
2. Draw

lin _ _ ger one moment in si _ lence to pray, For

gent _ _ ly, so gent _ ly, the rough _ ly made bier, Per _
near ye, the tru _ est, the fre _ est from guile, And

those who will sor _ row for him far a _ _ way; For

chance the freed spirit is hov _ er _ ing near, Then
kiss the cold lips that will nev _ er more smile; For that

*Bear Gently, So Gently, the Roughly Made Bier*

**4**

And while o'er his form peals the loud booming gun,
Remember that he hath his last battle won—
Hath conquered the foe the bravest may dread,
And the crown of the victor shall rest on his head.
Then on unto battle undaunted again,
Nor think ye one hero hath fallen in vain;
The blood of each martyr cries loudly to God,
And traitors shall bow 'neath his almighty rod,
And traitors shall bow 'neath his almighty rod.

J. Slinglandt. Engv.r & Pr.

To

Wm. Hayward Esq.

# Can I go dearest mother!

## Ballad

Composed by

# BERNARD COVERT.

Author of "The Sword of Bunker Hill," &c. &c.

3.

Published by S. Brainard's Sons Cleveland.

Entered according to act of Congress A.D. 1859 by H. Tolman & Co in the Clerk's Office of the Dist Court of Mass

# CAN I GO, DEAREST MOTHER?

Comp. by BERNARD COVERT.

VOICE.

PIANO.

1. I am
2. From the

writing to you mother, knowing well what you will say, When you
battered walls of Sumter, from the wild waves of the sea, I have

read with tear-ful fondness what I write to you to-day. Know-ing
heard her cry for suc-cor, as the voice of God to me; In pros-

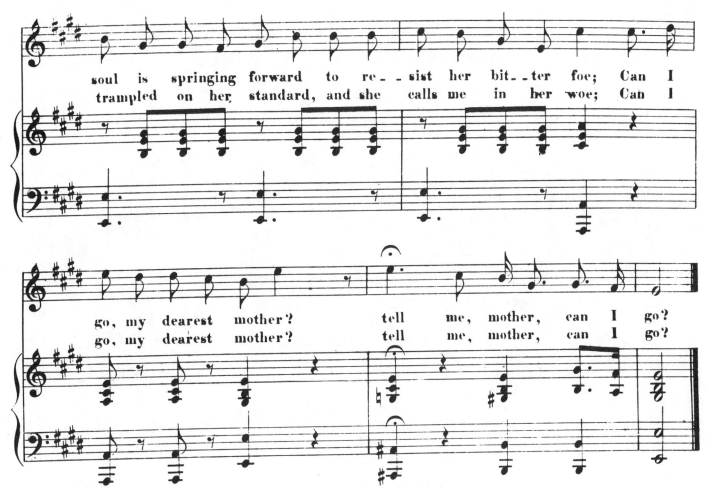

soul is springing forward to re___sist her bit__ter foe; Can I
trampled on her standard, and she calls me in her woe; Can I

go, my dearest mother? tell me, mother, can I go?
go, my dearest mother? tell me, mother, can I go?

3. I am young and slender, mother, they would call me yet a boy,
But I know the land I live in, and the blessings I enjoy;
I am old enough, my mother, to be loyal, proud and true
To be faithful to my country I have ever learned from you.
We must conquer this rebellion: let the doubting heart be still;
We must conquer it or perish. We must conquer, and we will!
But the faithful must not falter, and shall I be wanting? No!
  Bid me go, my dearest mother! tell me, mother, can I go!
4. He who led His chosen people, in their efforts to be free
From the tyranny of Egypt, will be merciful to me;
Will protect me by His power, whatso'er I undertake;
Will return me home in safety, dearest mother, for your sake.
Or should this, my bleeding country, need a victim such as me,
I am nothing more than others who have perished to be free,
On her bosom let me slumber; on her altar let me die;
  I am not afraid, my mother, in so good a cause to die.
5. There will come a day of gladness, when the people of the Lord
Shall look proudly on their banner, which His mercy has restored;
When the stars in perfect number, on their azure field of blue,
Shall be clustered in a Union, then and ever firm and true,
I may live to see it, mother, when the patriot's work is done,
And your heart so full of kindness, will beat proudly for your son;
Or through tears your eyes may see it with a sadly thoughtful view,
  And may love it still more dearly for the cost it won from you.
6. I have written to you, mother, with a consciousness of right
I am thinking of you fondly, with a loyal heart to-night:
When I have your noble bidding, which shall tell me to press on,
I will come and kiss you, mother, come and kiss you, and be gone
In the sacred name of Freedom, and my country as her due
In the name of Law and Justice, I have written this to you.
I am eager, anxious, longing to resist my country's foe;
  Shall I go, my dearest mother? tell me, mother, shall I go?

*Inscribed to*

SORROWING HEARTS AT HOME.

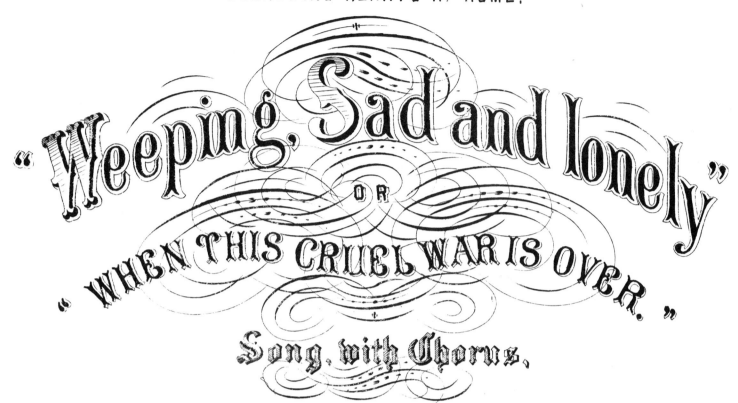

# "Weeping, Sad and lonely"

OR

## WHEN THIS CRUEL WAR IS OVER.

Song, with Chorus,

"Weeping, sad and lonely,
Hopes and fears, how vain,
When this cruel war is over,
Praying that we meet again."

WORDS BY

## Chas. Carroll Sawyer,

*Music Composed and Arranged by*

# HENRY TUCKER.

*Stackpole Sc*

Pr: 25 Cents.

BROOKLYN

Published by SAWYER & THOMPSON, 59 Fulton Av.

New-York.

HALL & SON

Phil.ª

LEE & WALKER.

Cleaveland. O.

S. BRAINARD & Cº

*Entered according to Act of Congress AD 1862 by Henry Tucker in the Clerk's Office of the District Court of the Southern District of New-York.*

# "WEEPING, SAD AND LONELY."

or

## "WHEN THIS CRUEL WAR IS OVER."

Words by CHAS. C. SAWYER.　　　　　　　Music by HENRY TUCKER.

*Moderato e cantabile.*

Dear-est love, do you re-mem-ber When we last did meet,

How you told me that you loved me, Kneel-ing at my feet?

Oh! how proud you stood be - fore me, In your suit of blue,

When you vow'd to me and country, Ev - er to be true.

**CHORUS.**

Weeping, sad and lone - ly, Hopes and fears, how vain.

Weeping, sad and lone - ly, Hopes and fears, how vain. Yet praying

Weeping, sad and lone - ly, Hopes and fears, how vain. Yet praying

When this cruel war is ov-er, Praying! that we meet a-gain.

**2.**

When the summer breeze is sighing,
  Mournfully, along !
Or when autumn leaves are falling,
  Sadly breathes the song.
Oft in dreams I see thee lying
  On the battle plain,
Lonely, wounded, even dying;
  Calling, but in vain.
   *CHORUS. Weeping, sad, &c.*

**3.**

If amid the din of battle,
  Nobly you should fall,
Far away from those who love you,
  None to hear you call.
Who would whisper words of comfort,
  Who would soothe your pain?
Ah! the many cruel fancies
  Ever in my brain.
   *CHORUS. Weeping, sad, &c.*

**4.**

But our country called you, darling,
  Angels cheer your way,
While our nation's sons are fighting,
  We can only pray.
Nobly strike for God and liberty,
  Let all nations see
How we love our starry banner,
  Emblem of the free.
   *CHORUS. Weeping, sad, &c.*

O COME YOU FROM THE

# BATTLE-FIELD ?

BY

Geo. F. Root.

Published by Root & Cady.

67 Washington St.

CHICAGO.

# "Oh, Come You from the Battle-Field?"

A Dialogue Duett for Soprano (in roman) and Tenor (in *italic.*)

Geo. F. Root.

Piano Forte.

*Moderato.*

1. "O come you from the bat - tle - field, and sol - dier can you tell  A-
3. "And do you know my Rob - ert now? O tell me, tell me true— Oh!
5. "Now sol - dier, bless - ings on your tongue; O Rob - ert could you know How
7. "Oh! is he real - ly com - ing home—and shall I real - ly see My

I've come from the bat-tle-field, I've come right from the war,   And
dame, he saved the colo-nel's life, And brave-ly it was done;   In
bronz'd, and tanned, and beard-ed, and you'd hard-ly know him, dame;   We've

well I know the Twen-ti-eth, and gal-lant lads they are—   From
his dis-patch they told it all, and nam'd and prais'd your son;   A
made your boy in-to a man, but yet his heart's the same;   For

colo-nel down to rank and file, I know my com-rades well,   And
med-al and a pen-sion's his— good luck to him I say,   And
oft-en still he talks of you, and al-ways to one tune—   But

news  I've  brought  for  you  good  dame,  your  Rob - ert  bade  me  tell."
he  has  not  a  com - rade  but  will  wish  him  well  to - day."
there,  I  will  not  tell  you  more,  for  he'll  be  with  you  soon."

*Tenor.*

O!  hap - py,  hap - py  meet - ing,  At  home,  at  home  once  more,  Give

*Soprano.*

O!  hap - py,  hap - py  meet - ing,  At  home,  at  home  once  more,  Give

joy - ful,  joy - ful  greet - ing,  All  sor - rows  now  are  o'er.

joy - ful,  joy - ful  greet - ing,  All  sor - rows  now  are  o'er.

To the

*Army & Navy*

OF THE UINON.

# When Johnny comes marching home

*Music introduced in the Soldier's Return March.*

BY

# GILMORE'S BAND

WORDS & MUSIC BY

# LOUIS LAMBERT.

③

BOSTON.
Published by Henry Tolman & Co. 291 Washington St.

Entered according to act of Congress AD 1863 by H. Tolman & Co. in the Clerk's office of the Dis.t Court of Mass.

# WHEN JOHNNY COMES MARCHING HOME.

With spirit.

Words and Music by LOUIS LAMBERT.

1. When Johnny comes marching home a-gain, Hur-rah, Hur-rah, We'll give him a hearty welcome then, Hur-rah, Hur-rah; The men will cheer, the boys will shout, The ladies, they will

2. The old church bell will peal with joy, Hur-rah, Hur-rah, To wel--come home our darling boy, Hur-rah, Hur-rah; The vil-lage lads and lassies say, With roses they will

all turn out, And we'll all feel gay, When Johnny comes marching home.
strew the way, And we'll all feel gay, When Johnny comes marching home.

3. Get rea _ dy for the Ju _ bi _ lee, Hur _ rah, Hur _
4. Let love and friendship on that day, Hur _ rah, Hur _

_ rah, We'll give the he _ ro three times three, Hurrah, Hur _ rah, The
_ rah, Their choic _ est treasures then display, Hurrah, Hur _ rah, And

laur_el wreath is rea_dy now, To place up_on his loyal brow, And we'll
let each one perform some part, To fill with joy the warriors heart, And we'll

all feel gay, When Johnny comes marching home.
all feel gay, When Johnny comes marching home.

THE VACANT CHAIR.

WITHIN SOUND OF THE ENEMY'S GUNS.

SILENT LUTE.

THE Vacant Chair

BY GEO. F. ROOT.

BATTLE CRY OF FREEDOM

WHO'LL SAVE THE LEFT

Published by Root & Cady.

95 Clark Street,

CHICAGO.

COPCUTT=WILLIAMS

# THE VACANT CHAIR;

## OR,

## WE SHALL MEET BUT WE SHALL MISS HIM.

### (THANKSGIVING, 1861.)

Words by H. S. W.

Music by G. F. ROOT.

1. We shall
2. At our
3. True they

meet,     but we shall miss him     There will be     one vacant chair;     We shall

fire - side, sad and lone - ly,     Oft - en will     the bosom swell     At re-

tell     us wreaths of glo - ry     Ev - er more     will deck his brow,     But this

lin - ger to ca - ress him While we breathe our evening prayer. When a
mem - brance of the sto - ry How our no - ble Wil-lie fell; How he
soothes the anguish on - ly Sweeping o'er our heartstrings now. Sleep to

year a - go we gathered, Joy was in his mild blue eye, But a
strove to bear our banner Thro' the thick - est of the fight, And up-
day, O ear - ly fall - en, In thy green and nar-row bed, Dirg - es

gold - en cord is sev - ered, And our hopes in ru - in lie.
hold our country's hon - or, In the strength of manhood's might.
from the pine and cypress Min - gle with the tears we shed.

## CHORUS.

We shall meet, but we shall miss him, There will be one vacant chair; We shall lin - ger to ca-

We shall meet, but we shall miss him, There will be one vacant chair; We shall lin - ger to ca-

ress him When we breathe our evening prayer.

ress him When we breathe our evening prayer.

DEDICATED TO THE SISTERS OF OUR VOLUNTEERS

# BRAVE BOYS are THEY

DUETT & CHORUS

FOR THE *Pianoforte*

POETRY & MUSIC BY

## HENRY CLAY WORK

*Author of*
"LOST ON THE LADY ELGIN"

CHICAGO

*Published by* H.M.HIGGINS 117 Randolph St.

Entd. according to act of Congress AD 1861 by H.M.Higgins in the Clerks office of the Dist Court for the Northn Dist of Ills.

# Brave Boys are They!

H. C. WORK

Not too fast.

Give the quarter notes their full time, with strongly marked accent.

Heav-i-ly falls the rain      Wild are the breez-es to- -night;      But

'neath the roof, the      hours as they fly,      Are hap-py, and calm, and bright.

Retard _____

Retard _____

**2**

Under the homestead roof
  Nestled so cozy and warm,
While soldiers sleep, with little or naught
  To shelter them from the storm.
Resting on grassy couches,
  Pillow'd on hillocks damp;
Of martial fare, how little we know,
  Till brothers are in the camp.
CHORUS        Brave boys &c.

**3**

Thinking no less of them,
  Loving our country the more,
We sent them forth to fight for the flag
  Their fathers before them bore.
Though the great tear drops started,
  This was our parting trust:
God bless you boys! we'll welcome you home
  When rebels are in the dust.
CHORUS        Brave boys &c.

**4**

May the bright wings of love
  Guard them wherever they roam;
The time has come when brothers must fight,
  And sisters must pray at home.
Oh! the dread field of battle!
  Soon to be strewn with graves!
If brothers fall, then bury them where
  Our banner in triumph waves.
CHORUS        Brave boys &c.

# Mother is the battle over?

Mother is the battle over,
Thousands have been killed they say:
Is my Father coming, tell me
Havr our soldiers gained the day?

*Composed by*

## B. E. ROEFS.

— ③ —

Boston
Published by Oliver Ditson & Co 277 Washington St
Firth.Pond & Co.   J.Church.Jr.   J.C.Haynes & Co.   J.E.Gould.   C.C.Clapp & Co.
N.York.        L'inn.         Boston.        Philad?         Boston

# MOTHER IS THE BATTLE OVER.

BENEDICT ROEFS.

Mother is the battle over! Mother is the battle over!

Thousands, thousands have been kill'd, they say; Is my Father coming! tell me,

Have our soldiers gain'd the day! Is he well or is he wounded! Mother do you

think he's slain! If you know, I pray you tell me, Will my father

come a-gain, will my fa - ther come a-gain!

Mother dear you're always sigh - ing

Since you last the paper read..... Tell me why you now are cry - ing

# GRAFTED INTO THE ARMY.

Words and Music by HENRY C. WORK.
No. 13.

Piano Forte.

1. Our Jim-my has gone for to live in a tent, They have graft-ed him in-to the
2. Drest up in his u-ni corn—dear lit-tle chap; They have graft-ed him in-to the
3. Now in my pro-vis-ions I see him re-vealed— They have graft-ed him in-to the

# JEFF IN PETTICOATS

## A Song for the times.

Entered according to Act of Congress, A.D.1865, by W. A. Pond, & C.º in the Clerk's Office of the District Court of the United States, for the Southern District of N.Y.

WORDS BY
# GEORGE COOPER.

MUSIC BY
# HENRY TUCKER.

Author of "Memory Bells." "Its all up in Dixie" &c &c.

Lith of H. C. Eno. 37 Park Row, N.Y.

NEW YORK,
Published by Wᵐ A POND & Cº 547 Broadway.

| Boston, | Rochester, | Chicago, | Buffalo, | Milwaukee, |
|---|---|---|---|---|
| O. Ditson & Cº | Joseph P. Shaw. | Root & Cady. | J. R. Blodgett. | H. N. Hempsted. |

# JEFF IN PETTICOATS.

Words by GEORGE COOPER.

Music by HENRY TUCKER.

1. Jeff Da - vis was a he - ro bold, you've heard of him, I know, He tried to make him - self a King where south - ern bree - zes
2. This Da - vis, he was al - ways full of blus - ter and of brag, He swore, on all our North - ern walls he'd plant his re - bel

blow; But "Un - cle Sam," he laid the youth a - cross his might - y knee, And
rag; But when to bat - tle he did go, he said, "I'm not so green, To

spanked him well, and that's the end of brave old Jef - fy D.
dodge the bul - lets, I will wear my tin - clad crin - o - line."

**CHORUS.**

AIR.

Oh! Jef - fy D! you "flow'r of chi - val - ree," Oh roy - al Jef - fy D! .......... your

ALTO.

TENOR.

Oh! Jef - fy D! you "flow'r of chi - val - ree," Oh roy - al Jef - fy D! .......... your

BASE.

Em - pire's but a tin - clad skirt, oh, charming Jef - fy D .

Em - pire's but a tin - clad skirt, oh, charming Jef - fy D .

**3.**

Now when he saw the game was up, he started for the woods,
His band-box hung upon his arm quite full of fancy goods :
Said Jeff. "They'll never take me now, I'm sure I'll not be seen,"
"They'd never think to look for me beneath my Crinoline."
     *Chorus.* Jeffy D ! &c.

**4.**

Jeff took with him, the people say, a mine of golden coin,
Which he from banks and other places, managed to purloin :
But while he ran, like every thief, he had to drop the spoons,
And may-be that's the reason why he dropped his pantaloons !
     *Chorus.* Jeffy D ! &c.

**5.**

Our Union boys were on his track for many nights and days,
His palpitating heart it beat, enough to burst his stays,
O ! what a dash he must have cut with form so tall and lean ;
Just fancy now the "What is it," dressed up in Crinoline !.
     *Chorus.* Jeffy D ! &c.

**6..**

The Ditch that Jeff was hunting for, he found was very near ;
He tried to "shift" his base again, his neck felt rather queer :
Just on the out-"skirts" of a wood his dainty shape was seen,
His boots stuck out, and now they'll hang old Jeff in Crinoline.
     *Chorus.* Jeffy D ! &c.

# THE NEW

# EMANCIPATION

# SONG:

## AS SUNG BY THE HUTCHINSON FAMILY,

MUSIC BY

# MRS. PARKHURST.

Author of the "Dying Drummer." "This hand never struck me, Mother." "Dost thou ever think of me love."
"Sanitary Fair Polka." "The new Emancipation Song." "Little Joe, the Contraband." "Sweet home of
my early days." Art thou thinking of me in my absence." &c. &c. Price, 30 cts. each.

 ⟨3⟩

## NEW YORK:

### Published by HORACE WATERS, No. 481 Broadway.

Boston: O. DITSON & Co., 277 Washington St.

Entered according to act of Congress A. D 1864, by Horace Waters, in the Clerk's office of the U. S. Dist. court for the Southern District of New York.

WARREN, Music Stereotyper, No. 43 Centre St., N. Y.

# THE NEW EMANCIPATION SONG.

Words by R. A. T.

Music by MRS. PARKHURST.

1. Oh! give the slaves their free - dom, You sure - ly do not need them, And no longer clothe and feed them, In these U - ni - ted States.

2. Then the slave no long - er be - labor, But act the part of neigh - bor, And hire white men to la - bor In these U - ni - ted States.

**3.**

Already the salvation
Of our slave holding nation
Demands the emancipation
Of slaves in the States.
      Cho.   For they all sigh, &c.


**4.**

Then renounce your cruel knavery
Of keeping men in slavery,
For its getting quite unsavory
E'en in the Border States.
      Cho.   For they all sigh, &c.


**5.**

Oh, let not our free soil
Be degraded by the toil
Of the men whom you despoil
In these United States.
      Cho.   For they all sigh, &c.


**6.**

Release from bondage dreary
Each darkey and his deary,
(And) (Don't) send them to Liberia
From these United States.
      Cho.   For they all sigh, &c.


**7.**

Esteem it but a fable,
That white men are not able
To take the place of sable
Slaves in the States.
      Cho.   For there's great cry, &c.


**8.**

And hire maids whose pretty faces
The rose and lily graces
To keep your pleasant places
In these United States.
      Cho.   For there's great cry, &c.


**9.**

If you wish to be commended
Let not Slavery be extended,
But its reign quickly ended
In these United States.
      Cho.   For they all sigh, &c.

THE VACANT CHAIR.

WITHIN SOUND OF THE ENEMY'S GUNS.

SILENT LUTE.

GLORY! GLORY!

OR THE

LITTLE OCTOROON.

SONG AND CHORUS.

BY

GEO. F. ROOT.

BATTLE CRY OF FREEDOM

WHO'LL SAVE THE LEFT

Published by Root & Cady.

67 Washington St.

CHICAGO.

COPCUTT-WILLIAMS

# GLORY! GLORY!

## OR THE

## LITTLE OCTOROON.

Words and Music by GEO. F. ROOT.

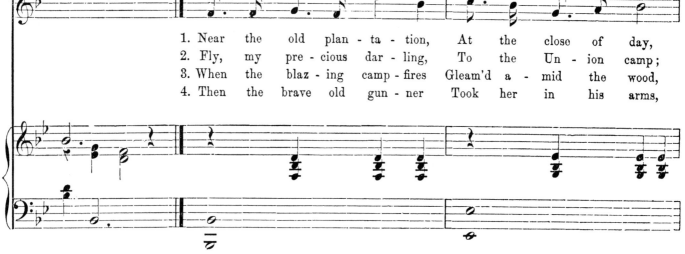

1. Near the old plan - ta - tion, At the close of day,
2. Fly, my pre - cious dar - ling, To the Un - ion camp;
3. When the blaz - ing camp - fires Gleam'd a - mid the wood,
4. Then the brave old gun - ner Took her in his arms,

Stood the wea - ry Moth - er and her child.
I will keep the hounds and hun - ters here.
And the boys were halt - ing for the night.
Think - ing of his own dear ones at home.

List - 'ning to the sounds A-
Go right through the for - est
In her won - d'rous beau - ty
And through all the march - es,

long the val - ley's way, While their hearts with hope were throb - bing wild!
Though 'tis dark and damp, God will keep you, dear one, nev - er fear.
Lit - tle Ro - sa stood Trem - bling and a - lone, be - fore their sight.
And their rude a - larms Safe - ly brought the lit - tle Oc - to - roon.

**CHORUS.**

Air

Glo - ry! glo - ry! How the Freed - men sang! Glo - ry! glo - ry! How the

Alto

Glo - ry! glo - ry! How the Freed - men sang! Glo - ry! glo - ry! How the

Tenor

Glo - ry! glo - ry! How the Freed - men sang! Glo - ry! glo - ry! How the

*Glory! Glory! (or The Little Octoroon)*  143

old woods rang! 'Twas the loy - al ar - my Sweep - ing to the sea,

old woods rang! 'Twas the loy - al ar - my Sweep - ing to the sea,

old woods rang! 'Twas the loy - al ar - my Sweep - ing to the sea,

Fling - ing out the ban - ner of the Free!

Fling - ing out the ban - ner of the Free, of the Free.

Fling - ing out the ban - ner of the Free!

Twentieth Edition.

# Kingdom Coming

## SONG AND CHORUS,

—BY—

# HENRY C. WORK.

AUTHOR OF

"Nellie Lost and Found;" "Our Captain's Last Words;" "Grafted into the Army, etc."

CHICAGO:

Published by ROOT & CADY, 95 Clark Street.

WM. HALL & SON, FIRTH, POND & CO., New York.   HENRY TOLMAN & CO., Boston.   S. BRAINARD & CO., Cleveland.

H. N. HEMPSTED, Milwaukee.   J. H. WHITTEMORE, Detroit.

# KINGDOM COMING.

Words and Music by HENRY C. WORK.

No. 10.

Piano-Forte.

1. Say, dar - keys, hab you seen de mas - sa, Wid de muff - stash on his face, Go long de road some time dis morn - in', Like he gwine to leab de place? He seen a smoke, way up de rib - ber, Whar de Link - um gum - boats lay; He took his hat, an' lef ber - ry sud - den, An' I

## CHORUS.

spec he's run a - way! De mas - sa run? ha, ha! De' dar - key stay? ho,

De mas - sa run? ha, ha! De dar - key stay? ho,

ho! It mus' be now de king - dom com - in', An' de year ob Ju - bi - lo!

ho! It mus' be now de king - dom com - in', An' de year ob Ju - bi - lo!

**Second Verse.**

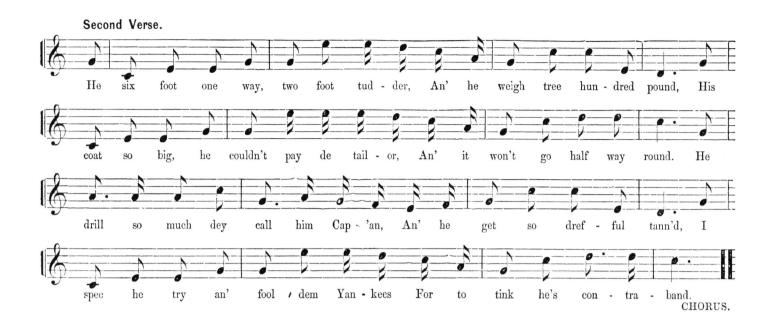

He six foot one way, two foot tud - der, An' he weigh tree hun - dred pound, His

coat so big, he couldn't pay de tail - or, An' it won't go half way round. He

drill so much dey call him Cap - 'an, An' he get so dref - ful tann'd, I

spec he try an' fool dem Yan - kees For to tink he's con - tra - band.
CHORUS.

**Third Verse.**

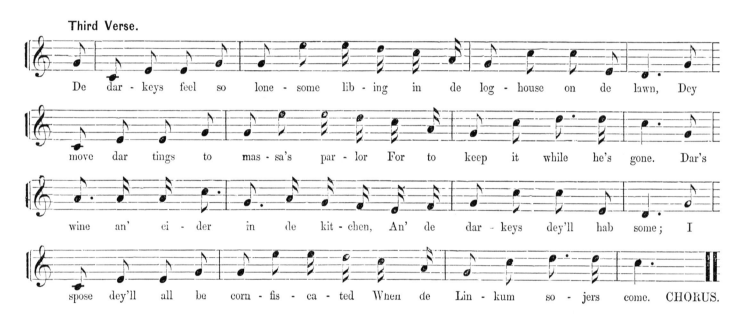

De dar - keys feel so lone - some lib - ing in de log - house on de lawn, Dey

move dar tings to mas - sa's par - lor For to keep it while he's gone. Dar's

wine an' ci - der in de kit - chen, An' de dar - keys dey'll hab some; I

spose dey'll all be corn - fis - ca - ted When de Lin - kum so - jers come. CHORUS.

**Fourth Verse.**

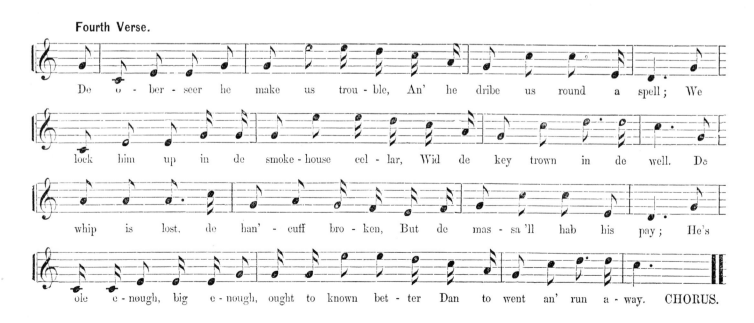

De o - ber - seer he make us trou - ble, An' he dribe us round a spell; We

lock him up in de smoke - house cel - lar, Wid de key trown in de well. De

whip is lost, de han' - cuff bro - ken, But de mas - sa 'll hab his pay; He's

ole e - nough, big e - nough, ought to known bet - ter Dan to went an' run a - way. CHORUS.

# '63

## IS THE

# JUBILEE.

## WORDS BY J. L. GREENE.

### MUSIC BY

# D. A. FRENCH.

### CHICAGO:

## PUBLISHED BY ROOT & CADY, 95 CLARK STREET.

H. TOLMAN & Co., Boston.        S. BRAINARD & CO., Cleveland.        H. N. HEMPSTED, Milwaukee.

# SIXTY-THREE IS THE JUBILEE.

Words by J. L. GREENE.

Music by D. A. FRENCH.

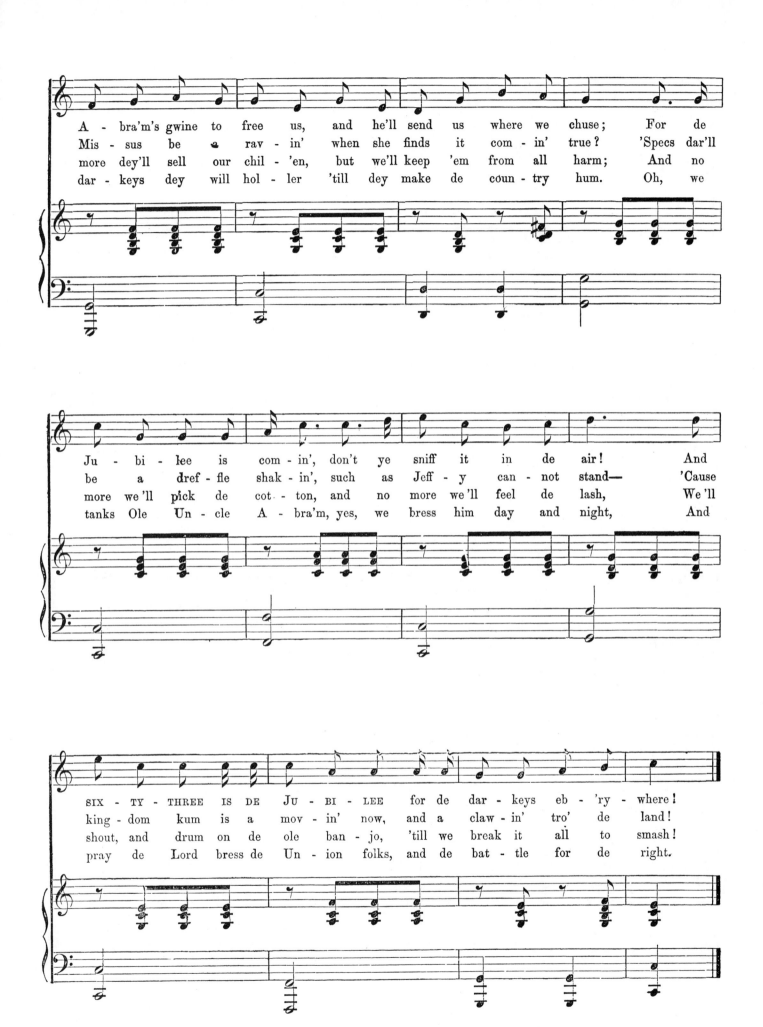

# WE ARE COMING FROM THE COTTON FIELDS.

Words by J C___N.

J. C. WALLACE.

*We Are Coming from the Cotton Fields*   155

## CHORUS.

Then come a-long my boys, Oh, come, come a-long, Then come a-long my brothers, Oh come, come a-

*156  We Are Coming from the Cotton Fields*